I0331121

C-1874 CAREER EXAMINATION SERIES

This is your PASSBOOK for...

Senior Account Clerk

Test Preparation Study Guide Questions & Answers

NLC®

NATIONAL LEARNING CORPORATION®

212 Michael Drive, Syosset, NY 11791
(516) 921-8888 • www.passbooks.com
E-mail: info@passbooks.com

PUBLISHED IN THE UNITED STATES OF AMERICA

PASSBOOK® SERIES

THE *PASSBOOK® SERIES* has been created to prepare applicants and candidates for the ultimate academic battlefield – the examination room.

At some time in our lives, each and every one of us may be required to take an examination – for validation, matriculation, admission, qualification, registration, certification, or licensure.

Based on the assumption that every applicant or candidate has met the basic formal educational standards, has taken the required number of courses, and read the necessary texts, the *PASSBOOK® SERIES* furnishes the one special preparation which may assure passing with confidence, instead of failing with insecurity. Examination questions – together with answers – are furnished as the basic vehicle for study so that the mysteries of the examination and its compounding difficulties may be eliminated or diminished by a sure method.

This book is meant to help you pass your examination provided that you qualify and are serious in your objective.

The entire field is reviewed through the huge store of content information which is succinctly presented through a provocative and challenging approach – the question-and-answer method.

A climate of success is established by furnishing the correct answers at the end of each test.

You soon learn to recognize types of questions, forms of questions, and patterns of questioning. You may even begin to anticipate expected outcomes.

You perceive that many questions are repeated or adapted so that you can gain acute insights, which may enable you to score many sure points.

You learn how to confront new questions, or types of questions, and to attack them confidently and work out the correct answers.

You note objectives and emphases, and recognize pitfalls and dangers, so that you may make positive educational adjustments.

Moreover, you are kept fully informed in relation to new concepts, methods, practices, and directions in the field.

You discover that you are actually taking the examination all the time: you are preparing for the examination by "taking" an examination, not by reading extraneous and/or supererogatory textbooks.

In short, this PASSBOOK®, used directedly, should be an important factor in helping you to pass your test.

SENIOR ACCOUNT CLERK

DUTIES
An employee in this class maintains a complex set of financial records, and compiles and prepares or assists a superior in preparing difficult and complex financial or statistical reports. Work may include utilization of computers or word processors with financial capabilities. In the absence of supervisory responsibilities, the assignment of positions to this class is based on the complexity of accounting records kept, and the amount of independent judgment exercised in the application of methods to particular problems. Supervision may be exercised over a number of clerical subordinates. Work is performed with relative technical independence and is reviewed by an administrative superior or professional accountant through verification of financial records and statements. Accounting records are also subject to audit by County and State auditors. Does related work as required.

EXAMPLES OF WORK:
Reviews a variety of more complex financial documents, classifies them and distributes items into a variety of accounts according to prescribed procedures and policies, and makes journal entries;
Posts figures to appropriate accounts, makes all necessary adjustments in balances and verifies and reconciles balances, renews status of accounts as adjustments are made, and takes appropriate action as authorizing payments, issuing checks, or preparing bills;
Tracks, audits, and monitors a variety of accounts, verifies adjustments are made to correct allocations, and issues reports as required;
May supervise employees by assigning and reviewing completed work and instructing new employees in specialized account-keeping activities;
Issues receipts for monies received and prepare funds for deposit into book accounts;
Reconciles accounts and prepares reports from information;
Contacts clients, vendors, or other agencies to obtain additional information;
Provides information orally or in writing in response to inquiries on status of accounts;
Compiles data for and prepares and analyzes complex financial and statistical records and reports;
Processes, sorts, indexes, records, and files a variety of control records and reports, or supervises the process;
Checks for accuracy of computations and completeness or supervises the preparation of daily, weekly and monthly reports which are compiled into summary reports or claims for state or federal reimbursement;
Prepares in final format, accounting and financial statements, payrolls, statistical tabulations and data, form letters, memoranda, vouchers, reports, requisitions or data from various equipment as the source material;
May assist in preparation of figures and reports for use in budget preparation;
May prepare, review, and process claims for State aid;
Does more complex payroll transactions and prepares all related reports;
Operates calculator, computer terminal, check writing machine, and other related office equipment.

SCOPE OF THE EXAMINATION
The written test will cover knowledge, skills and/or abilities in such areas as:
1. Fundamentals of account keeping and bookkeeping;
2. Understanding and interpreting written material;
3. Office record keeping; and
4. Name and number checking.

HOW TO TAKE A TEST

I. YOU MUST PASS AN EXAMINATION

A. WHAT EVERY CANDIDATE SHOULD KNOW

Examination applicants often ask us for help in preparing for the written test. What can I study in advance? What kinds of questions will be asked? How will the test be given? How will the papers be graded?

As an applicant for a civil service examination, you may be wondering about some of these things. Our purpose here is to suggest effective methods of advance study and to describe civil service examinations.

Your chances for success on this examination can be increased if you know how to prepare. Those "pre-examination jitters" can be reduced if you know what to expect. You can even experience an adventure in good citizenship if you know why civil service exams are given.

B. WHY ARE CIVIL SERVICE EXAMINATIONS GIVEN?

Civil service examinations are important to you in two ways. As a citizen, you want public jobs filled by employees who know how to do their work. As a job seeker, you want a fair chance to compete for that job on an equal footing with other candidates. The best-known means of accomplishing this two-fold goal is the competitive examination.

Exams are widely publicized throughout the nation. They may be administered for jobs in federal, state, city, municipal, town or village governments or agencies.

Any citizen may apply, with some limitations, such as the age or residence of applicants. Your experience and education may be reviewed to see whether you meet the requirements for the particular examination. When these requirements exist, they are reasonable and applied consistently to all applicants. Thus, a competitive examination may cause you some uneasiness now, but it is your privilege and safeguard.

C. HOW ARE CIVIL SERVICE EXAMS DEVELOPED?

Examinations are carefully written by trained technicians who are specialists in the field known as "psychological measurement," in consultation with recognized authorities in the field of work that the test will cover. These experts recommend the subject matter areas or skills to be tested; only those knowledges or skills important to your success on the job are included. The most reliable books and source materials available are used as references. Together, the experts and technicians judge the difficulty level of the questions.

Test technicians know how to phrase questions so that the problem is clearly stated. Their ethics do not permit "trick" or "catch" questions. Questions may have been tried out on sample groups, or subjected to statistical analysis, to determine their usefulness.

Written tests are often used in combination with performance tests, ratings of training and experience, and oral interviews. All of these measures combine to form the best-known means of finding the right person for the right job.

II. HOW TO PASS THE WRITTEN TEST

A. NATURE OF THE EXAMINATION

To prepare intelligently for civil service examinations, you should know how they differ from school examinations you have taken. In school you were assigned certain definite pages to read or subjects to cover. The examination questions were quite detailed and usually emphasized memory. Civil service exams, on the other hand, try to discover your present ability to perform the duties of a position, plus your potentiality to learn these duties. In other words, a civil service exam attempts to predict how successful you will be. Questions cover such a broad area that they cannot be as minute and detailed as school exam questions.

In the public service similar kinds of work, or positions, are grouped together in one "class." This process is known as *position-classification.* All the positions in a class are paid according to the salary range for that class. One class title covers all of these positions, and they are all tested by the same examination.

B. FOUR BASIC STEPS

1) Study the announcement

How, then, can you know what subjects to study? Our best answer is: "Learn as much as possible about the class of positions for which you've applied." The exam will test the knowledge, skills and abilities needed to do the work.

Your most valuable source of information about the position you want is the official exam announcement. This announcement lists the training and experience qualifications. Check these standards and apply only if you come reasonably close to meeting them.

The brief description of the position in the examination announcement offers some clues to the subjects which will be tested. Think about the job itself. Review the duties in your mind. Can you perform them, or are there some in which you are rusty? Fill in the blank spots in your preparation.

Many jurisdictions preview the written test in the exam announcement by including a section called "Knowledge and Abilities Required," "Scope of the Examination," or some similar heading. Here you will find out specifically what fields will be tested.

2) Review your own background

Once you learn in general what the position is all about, and what you need to know to do the work, ask yourself which subjects you already know fairly well and which need improvement. You may wonder whether to concentrate on improving your strong areas or on building some background in your fields of weakness. When the announcement has specified "some knowledge" or "considerable knowledge," or has used adjectives like "beginning principles of..." or "advanced ... methods," you can get a clue as to the number and difficulty of questions to be asked in any given field. More questions, and hence broader coverage, would be included for those subjects which are more important in the work. Now weigh your strengths and weaknesses against the job requirements and prepare accordingly.

3) Determine the level of the position

Another way to tell how intensively you should prepare is to understand the level of the job for which you are applying. Is it the entering level? In other words, is this the position in which beginners in a field of work are hired? Or is it an intermediate or advanced level? Sometimes this is indicated by such words as "Junior" or "Senior" in the class title. Other jurisdictions use Roman numerals to designate the level – Clerk I, Clerk II, for example. The word "Supervisor" sometimes appears in the title. If the level is not indicated by the title, check the description of duties. Will you be working under very close supervision, or will you have responsibility for independent decisions in this work?

4) Choose appropriate study materials

Now that you know the subjects to be examined and the relative amount of each subject to be covered, you can choose suitable study materials. For beginning level jobs, or even advanced ones, if you have a pronounced weakness in some aspect of your training, read a modern, standard textbook in that field. Be sure it is up to date and has general coverage. Such books are normally available at your library, and the librarian will be glad to help you locate one. For entry-level positions, questions of appropriate difficulty are chosen – neither highly advanced questions, nor those too simple. Such questions require careful thought but not advanced training.

If the position for which you are applying is technical or advanced, you will read more advanced, specialized material. If you are already familiar with the basic principles of your field, elementary textbooks would waste your time. Concentrate on advanced textbooks and technical periodicals. Think through the concepts and review difficult problems in your field.

These are all general sources. You can get more ideas on your own initiative, following these leads. For example, training manuals and publications of the government agency which employs workers in your field can be useful, particularly for technical and professional positions. A letter or visit to the government department involved may result in more specific study suggestions, and certainly will provide you with a more definite idea of the exact nature of the position you are seeking.

III. KINDS OF TESTS

Tests are used for purposes other than measuring knowledge and ability to perform specified duties. For some positions, it is equally important to test ability to make adjustments to new situations or to profit from training. In others, basic mental abilities not dependent on information are essential. Questions which test these things may not appear as pertinent to the duties of the position as those which test for knowledge and information. Yet they are often highly important parts of a fair examination. For very general questions, it is almost impossible to help you direct your study efforts. What we can do is to point out some of the more common of these general abilities needed in public service positions and describe some typical questions.

1) General information

Broad, general information has been found useful for predicting job success in some kinds of work. This is tested in a variety of ways, from vocabulary lists to questions about current events. Basic background in some field of work, such as sociology or economics, may be sampled in a group of questions. Often these are principles which have become familiar to most persons through exposure rather than through formal training. It is difficult to advise you how to study for these questions; being alert to the world around you is our best suggestion.

2) Verbal ability

An example of an ability needed in many positions is verbal or language ability. Verbal ability is, in brief, the ability to use and understand words. Vocabulary and grammar tests are typical measures of this ability. Reading comprehension or paragraph interpretation questions are common in many kinds of civil service tests. You are given a paragraph of written material and asked to find its central meaning.

3) Numerical ability

Number skills can be tested by the familiar arithmetic problem, by checking paired lists of numbers to see which are alike and which are different, or by interpreting charts and graphs. In the latter test, a graph may be printed in the test booklet which you are asked to use as the basis for answering questions.

4) Observation

A popular test for law-enforcement positions is the observation test. A picture is shown to you for several minutes, then taken away. Questions about the picture test your ability to observe both details and larger elements.

5) Following directions

In many positions in the public service, the employee must be able to carry out written instructions dependably and accurately. You may be given a chart with several columns, each column listing a variety of information. The questions require you to carry out directions involving the information given in the chart.

6) Skills and aptitudes

Performance tests effectively measure some manual skills and aptitudes. When the skill is one in which you are trained, such as typing or shorthand, you can practice. These tests are often very much like those given in business school or high school courses. For many of the other skills and aptitudes, however, no short-time preparation can be made. Skills and abilities natural to you or that you have developed throughout your lifetime are being tested.

Many of the general questions just described provide all the data needed to answer the questions and ask you to use your reasoning ability to find the answers. Your best preparation for these tests, as well as for tests of facts and ideas, is to be at your physical and mental best. You, no doubt, have your own methods of getting into an exam-taking mood and keeping "in shape." The next section lists some ideas on this subject.

IV. KINDS OF QUESTIONS

Only rarely is the "essay" question, which you answer in narrative form, used in civil service tests. Civil service tests are usually of the short-answer type. Full instructions for answering these questions will be given to you at the examination. But in case this is your first experience with short-answer questions and separate answer sheets, here is what you need to know:

1) Multiple-choice Questions

Most popular of the short-answer questions is the "multiple choice" or "best answer" question. It can be used, for example, to test for factual knowledge, ability to solve problems or judgment in meeting situations found at work.

A multiple-choice question is normally one of three types—

- It can begin with an incomplete statement followed by several possible endings. You are to find the one ending which *best* completes the statement, although some of the others may not be entirely wrong.
- It can also be a complete statement in the form of a question which is answered by choosing one of the statements listed.

- It can be in the form of a problem – again you select the best answer.

Here is an example of a multiple-choice question with a discussion which should give you some clues as to the method for choosing the right answer:

When an employee has a complaint about his assignment, the action which will *best* help him overcome his difficulty is to

A. discuss his difficulty with his coworkers
B. take the problem to the head of the organization
C. take the problem to the person who gave him the assignment
D. say nothing to anyone about his complaint

In answering this question, you should study each of the choices to find which is best. Consider choice "A" – Certainly an employee may discuss his complaint with fellow employees, but no change or improvement can result, and the complaint remains unresolved. Choice "B" is a poor choice since the head of the organization probably does not know what assignment you have been given, and taking your problem to him is known as "going over the head" of the supervisor. The supervisor, or person who made the assignment, is the person who can clarify it or correct any injustice. Choice "C" is, therefore, correct. To say nothing, as in choice "D," is unwise. Supervisors have and interest in knowing the problems employees are facing, and the employee is seeking a solution to his problem.

2) True/False Questions

The "true/false" or "right/wrong" form of question is sometimes used. Here a complete statement is given. Your job is to decide whether the statement is right or wrong.

SAMPLE: A roaming cell-phone call to a nearby city costs less than a non-roaming call to a distant city.

This statement is wrong, or false, since roaming calls are more expensive.

This is not a complete list of all possible question forms, although most of the others are variations of these common types. You will always get complete directions for answering questions. Be sure you understand *how* to mark your answers – ask questions until you do.

V. RECORDING YOUR ANSWERS

Computer terminals are used more and more today for many different kinds of exams.

For an examination with very few applicants, you may be told to record your answers in the test booklet itself. Separate answer sheets are much more common. If this separate answer sheet is to be scored by machine – and this is often the case – it is highly important that you mark your answers correctly in order to get credit.

An electronic scoring machine is often used in civil service offices because of the speed with which papers can be scored. Machine-scored answer sheets must be marked with a pencil, which will be given to you. This pencil has a high graphite content which responds to the electronic scoring machine. As a matter of fact, stray dots may register as answers, so do not let your pencil rest on the answer sheet while you are pondering the correct answer. Also, if your pencil lead breaks or is otherwise defective, ask for another.

Since the answer sheet will be dropped in a slot in the scoring machine, be careful not to bend the corners or get the paper crumpled.

The answer sheet normally has five vertical columns of numbers, with 30 numbers to a column. These numbers correspond to the question numbers in your test booklet. After each number, going across the page are four or five pairs of dotted lines. These short dotted lines have small letters or numbers above them. The first two pairs may also have a "T" or "F" above the letters. This indicates that the first two pairs only are to be used if the questions are of the true-false type. If the questions are multiple choice, disregard the "T" and "F" and pay attention only to the small letters or numbers.

Answer your questions in the manner of the sample that follows:

32. The largest city in the United States is
    A. Washington, D.C.
    B. New York City
    C. Chicago
    D. Detroit
    E. San Francisco

1) Choose the answer you think is best. (New York City is the largest, so "B" is correct.)
2) Find the row of dotted lines numbered the same as the question you are answering. (Find row number 32)
3) Find the pair of dotted lines corresponding to the answer. (Find the pair of lines under the mark "B.")
4) Make a solid black mark between the dotted lines.

VI. BEFORE THE TEST

Common sense will help you find procedures to follow to get ready for an examination. Too many of us, however, overlook these sensible measures. Indeed, nervousness and fatigue have been found to be the most serious reasons why applicants fail to do their best on civil service tests. Here is a list of reminders:

- Begin your preparation early – Don't wait until the last minute to go scurrying around for books and materials or to find out what the position is all about.
- Prepare continuously – An hour a night for a week is better than an all-night cram session. This has been definitely established. What is more, a night a week for a month will return better dividends than crowding your study into a shorter period of time.
- Locate the place of the exam – You have been sent a notice telling you when and where to report for the examination. If the location is in a different town or otherwise unfamiliar to you, it would be well to inquire the best route and learn something about the building.
- Relax the night before the test – Allow your mind to rest. Do not study at all that night. Plan some mild recreation or diversion; then go to bed early and get a good night's sleep.
- Get up early enough to make a leisurely trip to the place for the test – This way unforeseen events, traffic snarls, unfamiliar buildings, etc. will not upset you.
- Dress comfortably – A written test is not a fashion show. You will be known by number and not by name, so wear something comfortable.

- Leave excess paraphernalia at home – Shopping bags and odd bundles will get in your way. You need bring only the items mentioned in the official notice you received; usually everything you need is provided. Do not bring reference books to the exam. They will only confuse those last minutes and be taken away from you when in the test room.
- Arrive somewhat ahead of time – If because of transportation schedules you must get there very early, bring a newspaper or magazine to take your mind off yourself while waiting.
- Locate the examination room – When you have found the proper room, you will be directed to the seat or part of the room where you will sit. Sometimes you are given a sheet of instructions to read while you are waiting. Do not fill out any forms until you are told to do so; just read them and be prepared.
- Relax and prepare to listen to the instructions
- If you have any physical problem that may keep you from doing your best, be sure to tell the test administrator. If you are sick or in poor health, you really cannot do your best on the exam. You can come back and take the test some other time.

VII. AT THE TEST

The day of the test is here and you have the test booklet in your hand. The temptation to get going is very strong. Caution! There is more to success than knowing the right answers. You must know how to identify your papers and understand variations in the type of short-answer question used in this particular examination. Follow these suggestions for maximum results from your efforts:

1) Cooperate with the monitor

The test administrator has a duty to create a situation in which you can be as much at ease as possible. He will give instructions, tell you when to begin, check to see that you are marking your answer sheet correctly, and so on. He is not there to guard you, although he will see that your competitors do not take unfair advantage. He wants to help you do your best.

2) Listen to all instructions

Don't jump the gun! Wait until you understand all directions. In most civil service tests you get more time than you need to answer the questions. So don't be in a hurry. Read each word of instructions until you clearly understand the meaning. Study the examples, listen to all announcements and follow directions. Ask questions if you do not understand what to do.

3) Identify your papers

Civil service exams are usually identified by number only. You will be assigned a number; you must not put your name on your test papers. Be sure to copy your number correctly. Since more than one exam may be given, copy your exact examination title.

4) Plan your time

Unless you are told that a test is a "speed" or "rate of work" test, speed itself is usually not important. Time enough to answer all the questions will be provided, but this does not mean that you have all day. An overall time limit has been set. Divide the total time (in minutes) by the number of questions to determine the approximate time you have for each question.

5) Do not linger over difficult questions

If you come across a difficult question, mark it with a paper clip (useful to have along) and come back to it when you have been through the booklet. One caution if you do this – be sure to skip a number on your answer sheet as well. Check often to be sure that you have not lost your place and that you are marking in the row numbered the same as the question you are answering.

6) Read the questions

Be sure you know what the question asks! Many capable people are unsuccessful because they failed to *read* the questions correctly.

7) Answer all questions

Unless you have been instructed that a penalty will be deducted for incorrect answers, it is better to guess than to omit a question.

8) Speed tests

It is often better NOT to guess on speed tests. It has been found that on timed tests people are tempted to spend the last few seconds before time is called in marking answers at random – without even reading them – in the hope of picking up a few extra points. To discourage this practice, the instructions may warn you that your score will be "corrected" for guessing. That is, a penalty will be applied. The incorrect answers will be deducted from the correct ones, or some other penalty formula will be used.

9) Review your answers

If you finish before time is called, go back to the questions you guessed or omitted to give them further thought. Review other answers if you have time.

10) Return your test materials

If you are ready to leave before others have finished or time is called, take ALL your materials to the monitor and leave quietly. Never take any test material with you. The monitor can discover whose papers are not complete, and taking a test booklet may be grounds for disqualification.

VIII. EXAMINATION TECHNIQUES

1) Read the general instructions carefully. These are usually printed on the first page of the exam booklet. As a rule, these instructions refer to the timing of the examination; the fact that you should not start work until the signal and must stop work at a signal, etc. If there are any *special* instructions, such as a choice of questions to be answered, make sure that you note this instruction carefully.

2) When you are ready to start work on the examination, that is as soon as the signal has been given, read the instructions to each question booklet, underline any key words or phrases, such as *least*, *best*, *outline*, *describe* and the like. In this way you will tend to answer as requested rather than discover on reviewing your paper that you *listed without describing*, that you selected the *worst* choice rather than the *best* choice, etc.

3) If the examination is of the objective or multiple-choice type – that is, each question will also give a series of possible answers: A, B, C or D, and you are called upon to select the best answer and write the letter next to that answer on your answer paper – it is advisable to start answering each question in turn. There may be anywhere from 50 to 100 such questions in the three or four hours allotted and you can see how much time would be taken if you read through all the questions before beginning to answer any. Furthermore, if you come across a question or group of questions which you know would be difficult to answer, it would undoubtedly affect your handling of all the other questions.

4) If the examination is of the essay type and contains but a few questions, it is a moot point as to whether you should read all the questions before starting to answer any one. Of course, if you are given a choice – say five out of seven and the like – then it is essential to read all the questions so you can eliminate the two that are most difficult. If, however, you are asked to answer all the questions, there may be danger in trying to answer the easiest one first because you may find that you will spend too much time on it. The best technique is to answer the first question, then proceed to the second, etc.

5) Time your answers. Before the exam begins, write down the time it started, then add the time allowed for the examination and write down the time it must be completed, then divide the time available somewhat as follows:
   - If 3-1/2 hours are allowed, that would be 210 minutes. If you have 80 objective-type questions, that would be an average of 2-1/2 minutes per question. Allow yourself no more than 2 minutes per question, or a total of 160 minutes, which will permit about 50 minutes to review.
   - If for the time allotment of 210 minutes there are 7 essay questions to answer, that would average about 30 minutes a question. Give yourself only 25 minutes per question so that you have about 35 minutes to review.

6) The most important instruction is to *read each question* and make sure you know what is wanted. The second most important instruction is to *time yourself properly* so that you answer every question. The third most important instruction is to *answer every question.* Guess if you have to but include something for each question. Remember that you will receive no credit for a blank and will probably receive some credit if you write something in answer to an essay question. If you guess a letter – say "B" for a multiple-choice question – you may have guessed right. If you leave a blank as an answer to a multiple-choice question, the examiners may respect your feelings but it will not add a point to your score. Some exams may penalize you for wrong answers, so in such cases *only*, you may not want to guess unless you have some basis for your answer.

7) Suggestions
   a. Objective-type questions
      1. Examine the question booklet for proper sequence of pages and questions
      2. Read all instructions carefully
      3. Skip any question which seems too difficult; return to it after all other questions have been answered
      4. Apportion your time properly; do not spend too much time on any single question or group of questions

5. Note and underline key words – *all, most, fewest, least, best, worst, same, opposite,* etc.
6. Pay particular attention to negatives
7. Note unusual option, e.g., unduly long, short, complex, different or similar in content to the body of the question
8. Observe the use of "hedging" words – *probably, may, most likely,* etc.
9. Make sure that your answer is put next to the same number as the question
10. Do not second-guess unless you have good reason to believe the second answer is definitely more correct
11. Cross out original answer if you decide another answer is more accurate; do not erase until you are ready to hand your paper in
12. Answer all questions; guess unless instructed otherwise
13. Leave time for review

b. Essay questions
1. Read each question carefully
2. Determine exactly what is wanted. Underline key words or phrases.
3. Decide on outline or paragraph answer
4. Include many different points and elements unless asked to develop any one or two points or elements
5. Show impartiality by giving pros and cons unless directed to select one side only
6. Make and write down any assumptions you find necessary to answer the questions
7. Watch your English, grammar, punctuation and choice of words
8. Time your answers; don't crowd material

8) Answering the essay question

Most essay questions can be answered by framing the specific response around several key words or ideas. Here are a few such key words or ideas:

M's: manpower, materials, methods, money, management
P's: purpose, program, policy, plan, procedure, practice, problems, pitfalls, personnel, public relations

a. Six basic steps in handling problems:
1. Preliminary plan and background development
2. Collect information, data and facts
3. Analyze and interpret information, data and facts
4. Analyze and develop solutions as well as make recommendations
5. Prepare report and sell recommendations
6. Install recommendations and follow up effectiveness

b. Pitfalls to avoid
1. *Taking things for granted* – A statement of the situation does not necessarily imply that each of the elements is necessarily true; for example, a complaint may be invalid and biased so that all that can be taken for granted is that a complaint has been registered

2. *Considering only one side of a situation* – Wherever possible, indicate several alternatives and then point out the reasons you selected the best one
3. *Failing to indicate follow up* – Whenever your answer indicates action on your part, make certain that you will take proper follow-up action to see how successful your recommendations, procedures or actions turn out to be
4. *Taking too long in answering any single question* – Remember to time your answers properly

IX. AFTER THE TEST

Scoring procedures differ in detail among civil service jurisdictions although the general principles are the same. Whether the papers are hand-scored or graded by machine we have described, they are nearly always graded by number. That is, the person who marks the paper knows only the number – never the name – of the applicant. Not until all the papers have been graded will they be matched with names. If other tests, such as training and experience or oral interview ratings have been given, scores will be combined. Different parts of the examination usually have different weights. For example, the written test might count 60 percent of the final grade, and a rating of training and experience 40 percent. In many jurisdictions, veterans will have a certain number of points added to their grades.

After the final grade has been determined, the names are placed in grade order and an eligible list is established. There are various methods for resolving ties between those who get the same final grade – probably the most common is to place first the name of the person whose application was received first. Job offers are made from the eligible list in the order the names appear on it. You will be notified of your grade and your rank as soon as all these computations have been made. This will be done as rapidly as possible.

People who are found to meet the requirements in the announcement are called "eligibles." Their names are put on a list of eligible candidates. An eligible's chances of getting a job depend on how high he stands on this list and how fast agencies are filling jobs from the list.

When a job is to be filled from a list of eligibles, the agency asks for the names of people on the list of eligibles for that job. When the civil service commission receives this request, it sends to the agency the names of the three people highest on this list. Or, if the job to be filled has specialized requirements, the office sends the agency the names of the top three persons who meet these requirements from the general list.

The appointing officer makes a choice from among the three people whose names were sent to him. If the selected person accepts the appointment, the names of the others are put back on the list to be considered for future openings.

That is the rule in hiring from all kinds of eligible lists, whether they are for typist, carpenter, chemist, or something else. For every vacancy, the appointing officer has his choice of any one of the top three eligibles on the list. This explains why the person whose name is on top of the list sometimes does not get an appointment when some of the persons lower on the list do. If the appointing officer chooses the second or third eligible, the No. 1 eligible does not get a job at once, but stays on the list until he is appointed or the list is terminated.

X. HOW TO PASS THE INTERVIEW TEST

The examination for which you applied requires an oral interview test. You have already taken the written test and you are now being called for the interview test – the final part of the formal examination.

You may think that it is not possible to prepare for an interview test and that there are no procedures to follow during an interview. Our purpose is to point out some things you can do in advance that will help you and some good rules to follow and pitfalls to avoid while you are being interviewed.

What is an interview supposed to test?

The written examination is designed to test the technical knowledge and competence of the candidate; the oral is designed to evaluate intangible qualities, not readily measured otherwise, and to establish a list showing the relative fitness of each candidate – as measured against his competitors – for the position sought. Scoring is not on the basis of "right" and "wrong," but on a sliding scale of values ranging from "not passable" to "outstanding." As a matter of fact, it is possible to achieve a relatively low score without a single "incorrect" answer because of evident weakness in the qualities being measured.

Occasionally, an examination may consist entirely of an oral test – either an individual or a group oral. In such cases, information is sought concerning the technical knowledges and abilities of the candidate, since there has been no written examination for this purpose. More commonly, however, an oral test is used to supplement a written examination.

Who conducts interviews?

The composition of oral boards varies among different jurisdictions. In nearly all, a representative of the personnel department serves as chairman. One of the members of the board may be a representative of the department in which the candidate would work. In some cases, "outside experts" are used, and, frequently, a businessman or some other representative of the general public is asked to serve. Labor and management or other special groups may be represented. The aim is to secure the services of experts in the appropriate field.

However the board is composed, it is a good idea (and not at all improper or unethical) to ascertain in advance of the interview who the members are and what groups they represent. When you are introduced to them, you will have some idea of their backgrounds and interests, and at least you will not stutter and stammer over their names.

What should be done before the interview?

While knowledge about the board members is useful and takes some of the surprise element out of the interview, there is other preparation which is more substantive. It *is* possible to prepare for an oral interview – in several ways:

1) Keep a copy of your application and review it carefully before the interview

This may be the only document before the oral board, and the starting point of the interview. Know what education and experience you have listed there, and the sequence and dates of all of it. Sometimes the board will ask you to review the highlights of your experience for them; you should not have to hem and haw doing it.

2) Study the class specification and the examination announcement

Usually, the oral board has one or both of these to guide them. The qualities, characteristics or knowledges required by the position sought are stated in these documents. They offer valuable clues as to the nature of the oral interview. For example, if the job involves supervisory responsibilities, the announcement will usually indicate that knowledge of modern supervisory methods and the qualifications of the candidate as a supervisor will be tested. If so, you can expect such questions, frequently in the form of a hypothetical situation which you are expected to solve. NEVER go into an oral without knowledge of the duties and responsibilities of the job you seek.

3) Think through each qualification required

Try to visualize the kind of questions you would ask if you were a board member. How well could you answer them? Try especially to appraise your own knowledge and background in each area, *measured against the job sought*, and identify any areas in which you are weak. Be critical and realistic – do not flatter yourself.

4) Do some general reading in areas in which you feel you may be weak

For example, if the job involves supervision and your past experience has NOT, some general reading in supervisory methods and practices, particularly in the field of human relations, might be useful. Do NOT study agency procedures or detailed manuals. The oral board will be testing your understanding and capacity, not your memory.

5) Get a good night's sleep and watch your general health and mental attitude

You will want a clear head at the interview. Take care of a cold or any other minor ailment, and of course, no hangovers.

What should be done on the day of the interview?

Now comes the day of the interview itself. Give yourself plenty of time to get there. Plan to arrive somewhat ahead of the scheduled time, particularly if your appointment is in the fore part of the day. If a previous candidate fails to appear, the board might be ready for you a bit early. By early afternoon an oral board is almost invariably behind schedule if there are many candidates, and you may have to wait. Take along a book or magazine to read, or your application to review, but leave any extraneous material in the waiting room when you go in for your interview. In any event, relax and compose yourself.

The matter of dress is important. The board is forming impressions about you – from your experience, your manners, your attitude, and your appearance. Give your personal appearance careful attention. Dress your best, but not your flashiest. Choose conservative, appropriate clothing, and be sure it is immaculate. This is a business interview, and your appearance should indicate that you regard it as such. Besides, being well groomed and properly dressed will help boost your confidence.

Sooner or later, someone will call your name and escort you into the interview room. *This is it.* From here on you are on your own. It is too late for any more preparation. But remember, you asked for this opportunity to prove your fitness, and you are here because your request was granted.

What happens when you go in?

The usual sequence of events will be as follows: The clerk (who is often the board stenographer) will introduce you to the chairman of the oral board, who will introduce you to the other members of the board. Acknowledge the introductions before you sit down. Do not be surprised if you find a microphone facing you or a stenotypist sitting by. Oral interviews are usually recorded in the event of an appeal or other review.

Usually the chairman of the board will open the interview by reviewing the highlights of your education and work experience from your application – primarily for the benefit of the other members of the board, as well as to get the material into the record. Do not interrupt or comment unless there is an error or significant misinterpretation; if that is the case, do not hesitate. But do not quibble about insignificant matters. Also, he will usually ask you some question about your education, experience or your present job – partly to get you to start talking and to establish the interviewing "rapport." He may start the actual questioning, or turn it over to one of the other members. Frequently, each member undertakes the questioning on a particular area, one in which he is perhaps most competent, so you can expect each member to participate in the examination. Because time is limited, you may also expect some rather abrupt switches in the direction the questioning takes, so do not be upset by it. Normally, a board member will not pursue a single line of questioning unless he discovers a particular strength or weakness.

After each member has participated, the chairman will usually ask whether any member has any further questions, then will ask you if you have anything you wish to add. Unless you are expecting this question, it may floor you. Worse, it may start you off on an extended, extemporaneous speech. The board is not usually seeking more information. The question is principally to offer you a last opportunity to present further qualifications or to indicate that you have nothing to add. So, if you feel that a significant qualification or characteristic has been overlooked, it is proper to point it out in a sentence or so. Do not compliment the board on the thoroughness of their examination – they have been sketchy, and you know it. If you wish, merely say, "No thank you, I have nothing further to add." This is a point where you can "talk yourself out" of a good impression or fail to present an important bit of information. Remember, *you close the interview yourself.*

The chairman will then say, "That is all, Mr. ______, thank you." Do not be startled; the interview is over, and quicker than you think. Thank him, gather your belongings and take your leave. Save your sigh of relief for the other side of the door.

How to put your best foot forward

Throughout this entire process, you may feel that the board individually and collectively is trying to pierce your defenses, seek out your hidden weaknesses and embarrass and confuse you. Actually, this is not true. They are obliged to make an appraisal of your qualifications for the job you are seeking, and they want to see you in your best light. Remember, they must interview all candidates and a non-cooperative candidate may become a failure in spite of their best efforts to bring out his qualifications. Here are 15 suggestions that will help you:

1) Be natural – Keep your attitude confident, not cocky

If you are not confident that you can do the job, do not expect the board to be. Do not apologize for your weaknesses, try to bring out your strong points. The board is interested in a positive, not negative, presentation. Cockiness will antagonize any board member and make him wonder if you are covering up a weakness by a false show of strength.

2) Get comfortable, but don't lounge or sprawl

Sit erectly but not stiffly. A careless posture may lead the board to conclude that you are careless in other things, or at least that you are not impressed by the importance of the occasion. Either conclusion is natural, even if incorrect. Do not fuss with your clothing, a pencil or an ashtray. Your hands may occasionally be useful to emphasize a point; do not let them become a point of distraction.

3) Do not wisecrack or make small talk

This is a serious situation, and your attitude should show that you consider it as such. Further, the time of the board is limited – they do not want to waste it, and neither should you.

4) Do not exaggerate your experience or abilities

In the first place, from information in the application or other interviews and sources, the board may know more about you than you think. Secondly, you probably will not get away with it. An experienced board is rather adept at spotting such a situation, so do not take the chance.

5) If you know a board member, do not make a point of it, yet do not hide it

Certainly you are not fooling him, and probably not the other members of the board. Do not try to take advantage of your acquaintanceship – it will probably do you little good.

6) Do not dominate the interview

Let the board do that. They will give you the clues – do not assume that you have to do all the talking. Realize that the board has a number of questions to ask you, and do not try to take up all the interview time by showing off your extensive knowledge of the answer to the first one.

7) Be attentive

You only have 20 minutes or so, and you should keep your attention at its sharpest throughout. When a member is addressing a problem or question to you, give him your undivided attention. Address your reply principally to him, but do not exclude the other board members.

8) Do not interrupt

A board member may be stating a problem for you to analyze. He will ask you a question when the time comes. Let him state the problem, and wait for the question.

9) Make sure you understand the question

Do not try to answer until you are sure what the question is. If it is not clear, restate it in your own words or ask the board member to clarify it for you. However, do not haggle about minor elements.

10) Reply promptly but not hastily

A common entry on oral board rating sheets is "candidate responded readily," or "candidate hesitated in replies." Respond as promptly and quickly as you can, but do not jump to a hasty, ill-considered answer.

11) Do not be peremptory in your answers

A brief answer is proper – but do not fire your answer back. That is a losing game from your point of view. The board member can probably ask questions much faster than you can answer them.

12) Do not try to create the answer you think the board member wants

He is interested in what kind of mind you have and how it works – not in playing games. Furthermore, he can usually spot this practice and will actually grade you down on it.

13) Do not switch sides in your reply merely to agree with a board member

Frequently, a member will take a contrary position merely to draw you out and to see if you are willing and able to defend your point of view. Do not start a debate, yet do not surrender a good position. If a position is worth taking, it is worth defending.

14) Do not be afraid to admit an error in judgment if you are shown to be wrong

The board knows that you are forced to reply without any opportunity for careful consideration. Your answer may be demonstrably wrong. If so, admit it and get on with the interview.

15) Do not dwell at length on your present job

The opening question may relate to your present assignment. Answer the question but do not go into an extended discussion. You are being examined for a *new* job, not your present one. As a matter of fact, try to phrase ALL your answers in terms of the job for which you are being examined.

Basis of Rating

Probably you will forget most of these "do's" and "don'ts" when you walk into the oral interview room. Even remembering them all will not ensure you a passing grade. Perhaps you did not have the qualifications in the first place. But remembering them will help you to put your best foot forward, without treading on the toes of the board members.

Rumor and popular opinion to the contrary notwithstanding, an oral board wants you to make the best appearance possible. They know you are under pressure – but they also want to see how you respond to it as a guide to what your reaction would be under the pressures of the job you seek. They will be influenced by the degree of poise you display, the personal traits you show and the manner in which you respond.

ABOUT THIS BOOK

This book contains tests divided into Examination Sections. Go through each test, answering every question in the margin. We have also attached a sample answer sheet at the back of the book that can be removed and used. At the end of each test look at the answer key and check your answers. On the ones you got wrong, look at the right answer choice and learn. Do not fill in the answers first. Do not memorize the questions and answers, but understand the answer and principles involved. On your test, the questions will likely be different from the samples. Questions are changed and new ones added. If you understand these past questions you should have success with any changes that arise. Tests may consist of several types of questions. We have additional books on each subject should more study be advisable or necessary for you. Finally, the more you study, the better prepared you will be. This book is intended to be the last thing you study before you walk into the examination room. Prior study of relevant texts is also recommended. NLC publishes some of these in our Fundamental Series. Knowledge and good sense are important factors in passing your exam. Good luck also helps. So now study this Passbook, absorb the material contained within and take that knowledge into the examination. Then do your best to pass that exam.

EXAMINATION SECTION

EXAMINATION SECTION

TEST 1

DIRECTIONS: Each question or incomplete statement is followed by several suggested answers or completions. Select the one that BEST answers the question or completes the statement. *PRINT THE LETTER OF THE CORRECT ANSWER IN THE SPACE AT THE RIGHT.*

Questions 1-5.

DIRECTIONS: Questions 1 through 5 are to be answered on the basis of the extracts from Federal income tax withholding and Social Security tax tables shown below. These tables indicate the amounts which must be withheld from the employee's salary by his employer for Federal income tax and for Social Security. They are based on weekly earnings.

INCOME TAX WITHHOLDING TABLE							
The wages are		And the number of withholding allowances is					
At Least	But Less Than	5	6	7	8	9	10 or More
		The amount of income tax to be withheld shall be					
$300	$320	$24.60	$19.00	$13.80	$ 8.60	$4.00	$ 0
320	340	28.80	22.80	17.40	12.20	7.00	2.80
340	360	33.00	27.00	21.00	15.80	10.60	5.60
360	380	37.20	31.20	25.20	19.40	14.20	9.00
380	400	41.40	34.40	29.40	23.40	17.80	12.60
400	420	45.60	39.60	33.60	27.60	21.40	16.20
420	440	49.80	43.80	37.80	31.80	25.60	19.80
440	460	54.00	48.00	42.00	36.00	29.80	23.80
460	480	58.20	52.20	46.20	40.20	34.00	38.00
480	500	62.40	46.40	40.40	44.40	38.20	32.20

SOCIAL SECURITY TABLE					
WAGES			WAGES		
At Least	But Less Than	Tax to be Withheld	At Least	But Less Than	Tax to be Withheld
$333.18	$333.52	$19.50	$336.60	$336.94	$19.70
333.52	333.86	19.52	336.94	337.28	19.72
333.86	334.20	19.54	337.28	337.62	19.74
334.20	334.54	19.56	337.62	337.96	19.76
334.54	334.88	19.58	337.96	338.30	19.78
334.88	335.22	19.60	338.30	338.64	19.80
335.22	335.56	19.62	338.64	338.98	19.82
335.56	335.90	19.64	338.98	339.32	19.84
335.90	336.24	19.66	339.32	339.66	19.86
336.24	336.60	19.68	339.66	340.00	19.88

1. If an employee has a weekly wage of $379.50 and claims 6 withholding allowances, the amount of income tax to be withheld is 1.____
   A. $27.00 B. $31.20 C. $35.40 D. $37.20

2. An employee had wages of $335.60 for one week. 2.____
   With eight withholding allowances claimed, how much income tax will be withheld from his salary?
   A. $8.60 B. $12.00 C. $13.80 D. $17.40

3. How much social security tax will an employee with weekly wages of $335.60 pay? 3.____
   A. $19.60 B. $19.62 C. $19.64 D. $19.66

4. Mr. Wise earns $339.80 a week and claims seven withholding allowances. 4.____
   What is his take-home pay after income tax and social security tax are deducted?
   A. $300.32 B. $302.52 C. $319.92 D. $322.40

5. If an employee pays $19.74 in social security tax and claims eight withholding allowances, the amount of income tax that should be withheld from his wages is 5.____
   A. $8.60 B. $12.20 C. $13.80 D. $15.80

6. A fundamental rule of bookkeeping states that an individual's assets equal his liabilities plus his proprietorship (ASSETS = LIABILITIES – PROPRIETORSHIP). Which of the following statements logically follows from this rule? 6.____
   A. ASSETS = PROPRIETORSHIP – LIABILITIES
   B. LIABILITIES = ASSETS + PROPRIETORSHIP
   C. PROPRIETORSHIP = ASSETS – LIABILITIES
   D. PROPRIETORSHIP = LIABILITIES + ASSETS

7. Mr. Martin's assets consist of the following: 7.____

Cash on Hand:	$5,233.74
Furniture:	$4,925.00
Government Bonds:	$5,500.00

   What are his TOTAL assets?
   A. $10,158.74 $10,425.00 C. $10,733.74 D. $15,658.74

8. If Mr. Mitchell has $627.04 in his checking account and then writes three checks for $241.74, $13.24, and $101.97, what will be his new balance? 8.____
   A. $257.88 B. $269.08 C. $357.96 D. $368.96

9. An employee's net pay is equal to his total earnings less all deductions. 9.____
   If an employee's total earnings in a pay period are $497.05, what is his NET pay if he has the following deductions: Federal income tax, $90.32; FICA: $28.74; State tax: $18.79; City tax: $7.25; Pension: $1.88?
   A. $351.17 B. $351.07 C. $350.17 D. $350.07

10. A petty cash fund had an opening balance of $85.75 on December 1. Expenditures of $23.00, $15.65, $5.23, $14.75, and $26.38 were made out of his fund during the first 14 days of the month. Then, on December 17, another $38.50 was added to the fund. 10.____
If additional expenditures of $17.18, $3.29, and $11.64 were made during the remainder of the month, what was the FINAL balance of the petty cash fund at the end of December?
A. $6.93 B. $7.13 C. $46.51 D. $91.40

Questions 11-15.

DIRECTIONS: Questions 11 through 15 are to be answered on the basis of the following instructions.

The chart below is used by the loan division of a city retirement system for the following purposes: (1) to calculate the monthly payment a member must pay on an outstanding loan; (2) to calculate how much a member owes on an outstanding loan after he has made a number of payments.

To calculate the amount a member must pay each month in repaying his loan, look at Column II on the chart. You will notice that each entry in Column II corresponds to a number appearing under the *Months* column; for example, 1.004868 corresponds to 1 month, 0.503654 corresponds to 2 months, etc. To calculate the amount a member must pay each month, use the following procedure: multiply the amount of the load by the entry in Column II which corresponds to the number of months over which the load will be paid back. For example, if a loan of $200 is taken out for six months, multiply $200 by 0.169518, the entry in Column II which corresponds to six months.

In order to calculate the balance still owed on an outstanding loan, multiply the monthly payment by the number in Column I which corresponds to the number of monthly payments which remain to be paid on the loan. For example, if a member is supposed to pay $106.00 a month for twelve months, after seven payments, five monthly payments remain. To calculate the balance owed on the loan at this point, multiply the $106.00 monthly payment by 4.927807, the number in Column I that corresponds to five months.

Months	Column I	Column II
1	0.995156	1.004868
2	1.985491	0.503654
3	2.971029	0.336584
4	3.951793	0.253050
5	4.927807	0.202930
6	5.899092	0.169518
7	6.865673	0.145652
8	7.827572	0.127754
9	8.784811	0.113833
10	9.737414	0.102697
11	10.685402	0.093586
12	11.628798	0.085994
13	12.567624	0.079570
14	13.501902	0.074064
15	14.431655	0.069292

11. If Mr. Carson borrows $1,500 for eight months, how much will he have to pay back each month? 11.____
    A. $187.16 B. $191.63 C. $208.72 D. $218.65

12. If a member borrows $2,400 for one year, the amount he will have to pay back each month is 12.____
    A. $118.78 B. $196.18 C. $202.28 D. $206.38

13. Mr. Elliott borrowed $1,700 for a period of fifteen months. Each month he will have to pay back 13.____
    A. $117.80 B. $116.96 C. $107.79 D. $101.79

14. Mr. Aylward is paying back a thirteen-month loan at the rate of $173.13 a month. 14.____
    If he has already made six monthly payments, how much does he owe on the outstanding loan?
    A. $1,027.38 B. $1,178.75 C. $1,188.65 D. $1,898.85

15. A loan was taken out for 15 months, and the monthly payment was $104.75. After two monthly payments, how much was still owed on this load? 15.____
    A. $515.79 B. $863.89 C. $1,116.76 D. $1,316.46

16. The ABC Corporation had a gross income of $125,500.00 in 2015. Of this, it paid 60% for overhead. 16.____
    If the gross income for 2016 increased by $6,500 and the cost of overhead increased to 61% of gross income, how much more did it pay for overhead in 2016 than in 2015?
    A. $1,320 B. $5,220 C. $7,530 D. $8,052

17. After one year, Mr. Richards paid back a total of $1,695.00 as payment for a $1,500.00 loan. All the money paid over $1,500.00 was simple interest. The interest charge was MOST NEARLY 17.____
A. 13% B. 11% C. 9% D. 7%

18. A checking account has a balance of $253.36. 18.____
If deposits of $36.95, $210.23, and $7.34 and withdrawals of $117.35, $23.37, and $15.98 are made, what is the NEW balance of the account?
A. $155.54 B. $351.18 C. $364.58 D. $664.58

19. In 2015, the W Realty Company spent 27% of its income on rent. 19.____
If it earned $97,254.00 in 2015, the amount it paid for rent was
A. $26.258.58 B. $26,348.58 C. $27,248.58 D. $27,358.58

20. Six percent simple annual interest on $2,436.18 is MOST NEARLY 20.____
A. $145.08 B. $145.17 c. $146.08 D. $146.17

21. Assume that the XYZ Company has $10,402.72 cash on hand. 21.____
If it pays $699.83 of this for rent, the amount of cash on hand would be
A. $9,792.89 B. $9,702.89 C. $9,692.89 D. $9,602.89

22. On January 31, Mr. Warren's checking account had a balance of $933.68. 22.____
If he deposited $36.40 on February 2, $126.00 on February 9, and $90.02 on February 16 and wrote no checks during this period, what was the balance of his account on February 17?
A. $680.26 B. $681.26 C. $1,186.10 D. $1,187.00

23. Multiplying a number by .75 is the same as 23.____
A. multiplying it by 2/3
B. dividing it by 2/3
C. multiplying it by 3/4
D. dividing it by 3/4

24. In City Agency A, 2/3 of the employees are enrolled in a retirement system. 24.____
City Agency B has the same number of employees as Agency A, and 60% of these are enrolled in a retirement system.
If Agency A has a total of 660 employees, how many MORE employees does it have enrolled in a retirement system than does Agency B?
B. 36 B. 44 C. 56 D. 66

25. Net Worth is equal to Assets minus Liabilities. 25.____
If, at the end of year, a textile company had assets of $98,695.83 and liabilities of $59,238.29, what was its net worth?
A. $38,478.54 B. $38,488.64 C. $39,457.54 D. $48,557.54

KEY (CORRECT ANSWERS)

1.	B	11.	B
2.	B	12.	D
3.	C	13.	A
4.	B	14.	C
5.	B	15.	D
6.	C	16.	B
7.	D	17.	A
8.	B	18.	B
9.	D	19.	A
10.	B	20.	D
21.	B		
22.	C		
23.	C		
24.	B		
25.	C		

TEST 2

DIRECTIONS: Each question or incomplete statement is followed by several suggested answers or completions. Select the one that BEST answers the question or completes the statement. *PRINT THE LETTER OF THE CORRECT ANSWER IN THE SPACE AT THE RIGHT.*

Questions 1-10.

DIRECTIONS: Questions 1 through 10 below present the identification numbers, initials, and last names of employees enrolled in a city retirement system. You are to choose the option (A, B, C, or D) that has the IDENTICAL identification number, initials, and last name as those given in each question.

<u>Sample Question</u>
B145698 JL Jones

A. B146798 JL Jones B. B145698 JL Jonas
C. P145698 JL Jones D. B145698 JL Jones

The correct answer is D. Only Option D shows the identification number, initials, and last name exactly as they are in the sample question. Options A, B, and C have errors in the identification number or last name.

1. J297483 PL Robinson 1.____
   A. J294783 PL Robinson B. J297483 PL Robinson
   C. J297483 Pl Robinson D. J297843 PL Robinson

2. S497662 JG Schwartz 2.____
   B. S497662 JG Schwarz B. S497762 JG Schwartz
   C. S497662 JG Schwartz D. S497663 JG Schwartz

3. G696436 LN Alberton 3.____
   A. G696436 LM Alberton B. G696436 LN Albertson
   C. G696346 LN Albertson D. G696436 LN Alberton

4. R774923 AD Aldrich 4.____
   A. R774923 AD Aldrich B. R744923 AD Aldrich
   C. R774932 AP Aldrich D. R774932 AD Allrich

5. N239638 RP Hrynyk 5.____
   A. N236938 PR Hrynyk B. N236938 RP Hrynyk
   C. N239638 PR Hrynyk D. N239638 Hrynyk

6. R156949 LT Carlson 6.____
   A. R156949 LT Carlton B. R156494 LT Carlson
   C. R159649 LT Carlton D. R156949 LT Carlson

7. T524697 MN Orenstein 7.____
   A. T524697 MN Orenstein B. T524967 MN Orinstein
   C. T524697 NM Ornstein D. T524967 NM Orenstein

8. L346239 JD Remsen 8.____
   A. L346239 JD Remson
   B. L364239 JD Remsen
   C. L346329 JD Remsen
   D. L346239 JD Remsen

9. P966438 SB Rieperson 9.____
   A. P996438 SB Rieperson
   B. P466438 SB Reiperson
   C. R996438 SB Rieperson
   D. P966438 SB Rieperson

10. D749382 CD Thompson 10.____
   A. P749382 CD Thompson
   B. D749832 CD Thomsonn
   C. D749382 CD Thompson
   D. D749823 CD Thomspon

Questions 11-20.

DIRECTIONS: Assume that each of the capital letters in the table below represents the name of an employee enrolled in the city's employees' personnel system. The number directly beneath the letter represents the agency for which the employee works, and the small letter directly beneath represents the code for the employee's account.

Name of Employee	L	O	T	Q	A	M	R	N	C
Agency	3	4	5	9	8	7	2	1	6
Account Code	r	f	b	i	d	t	g	e	n

In each of the following Questions 11 through 20, the agency code numbers and the account code letters in Columns 2 and 3 should correspond to the capital letters in Column 1 and should be in the same consecutive order. For each question, look at each column carefully and mark your answer as follows:

If there are one or more errors in Column 2 only, mark your answer A.
If there are one or more errors in Column 3 only, mark your answer B.
I there are one or more errors in Column 2 and one or more errors in Column 3, mark your answer C.
If there are NO errors in either column, mark your answer D.

Sample Question

Column 1	Column 2	Column 3
TQLMOC	583746	birtfn

In Column 2, the second agency code number (corresponding to letter Q) should be 9, not 8. Column 3 is coded correctly to Column 1. Since there is an error only in Column 2, the correct answer is A.

	COLUMN 1	COLUMN 2	COLUMN 3	
11.	QLNRCA	931268	iregnd	11.____
12.	NRMOTC	127546	egftbn	12.____
13.	RCTALM	265837	gndbrt	13.____
14.	TAMLON	578341	bdtrfe	14.____
15.	ANTORM	815427	debigt	15.____
16.	MRALON	728341	tgdrfe	16.____
17.	CTNQRO	657924	ndeigf	17.____
18.	QMROTA	972458	itgfbd	18.____
19.	RQMCOL	297463	gitnfr	19.____
20.	NOMRTQ	147259	eftgbi	20.____

Questions 21-25.

DIRECTIONS: Questions 21 through 25 are to be answered SOLELY on the basis of the following passage.

The city may issue its own bonds or it may purchase bonds as an investment. Bonds may be issued in various denominations, and the face value of the bond is its par value. Before purchasing a bond, the investor desires to know the rate of income that the investment may yield in computing the yield on a bond, it is assumed that the investor will keep the bond until the date of maturity, except for callable bonds which are not considered in this passage. To compute exact yield is a complicated mathematical problem, and scientifically prepared tables are generally used to avoid such computation. However, the approximate yield can be computed much more easily. In computing approximate yield, the accrued interest on the date of purchase should be ignored because the buyer who pays accrued interest to the seller receives it again at the next interest date. Bonds bought at a premium (which cost more) yield a lower rate of income than the same bonds bought at par (face value), and bounds bought at a discount (which cost less) yield a higher rate of income than the same bonds bought at par.

21. An investor bought a $10,000 city bond paying 6% interest. Which of the following purchase prices would indicate that the bond was bought at a premium? 21.____
    A. $9,000 B. $9,400 C. $10,000 D. $10,600

22. During 2016, a particular $10,000 bond paying 7 ½% sold at fluctuating prices. Which of the following prices would indicate that the bond was bought at a discount? 22.____
    A. $9,800 B. $10,000 C. $10,200 D. $10,750

23. A certain group of bonds was sold in denominations of$5,000, $10,000, $20,000, and $50,000. 23.____
In the following list of four purchase prices, which one is MOST likely to represent a bond sold at par value?
A. $10,500 B. $20,000 C. $22,000 D. $49,000

24. When computing the approximate yield on a bond, it is DESIRABLE to 24.____
A. assume the bond was purchased at par
B. consult scientifically prepared tables
C. ignore accrued interest on the date of purchase
D. wait until the bond reaches maturity

25. Which of the following is MOST likely to be an exception to the information provided in the above passage? 25.____
Bonds
A. purchased at a premium
B. sold at par
C. sold before maturity
D. which are callable

KEY (CORRECT ANSWERS)

1.	B	11.	D
2.	C	12.	C
3.	D	13.	B
4.	A	14.	A
5.	D	15.	B
6.	D	16.	D
7.	A	17.	C
8.	D	18.	D
9.	D	19.	A
10.	C	20.	D

21. D
22. A
23. B
24. C
25. D

TEST 3

DIRECTIONS: Each question or incomplete statement is followed by several suggested answers or completions. Select the one that BEST answers the question or completes the statement. *PRINT THE LETTER OF THE CORRECT ANSWER IN THE SPACE AT THE RIGHT.*

Questions 1-6.

DIRECTIONS: Questions 1 through 6 consist of computations of addition, subtraction, multiplication, and division. For each question, do the computation indicated, and choose the correct answer from the four choices given.

1. ADD: 8936 7821 8953 4297 9785 6579 1.____

A. 45371 B. 45381 C. 46371 D. 46381

2. SUBTRACT: 95,432 67,596 2.____

A. 27,836 B. 27,846 C. 27,936 D. 27,946

3. MULTIPLY: 987 867 3.____

A. 854609 B. 854729 C. 855709 D. 855729

4. DIVIDE: 59)321439.0 4.____

A. 5438.1 B. 5447.1 C. 5448.1 D. 5457.1

5. DIVIDE: .057)721 5.____

A. 12,648.0 B. 12,648.1 C. 12,649.0 D. 12,649.1

6. ADD: 1/2 + 5/7 6.____
A. 1 3/14 B. 1 2/7 C. 1 5/14 D. 1 3/7

7. If the total number of employees in one city agency increased from 1,927 to 2,006 during a certain year, the percentage increase in the number of employees for that year is MOST NEARLY 7.____
A. 4% B. 5% C. 6% D. 7%

8. During a single fiscal year, which totaled 248 workdays, one account clerk verified 1,488 purchase vouchers. 8.____
Assuming a normal work week of five days, what is the average number of vouchers verified by the account clerk in a one-week period during this fiscal year?
   A. 25 B. 30 C. 35 D. 40

9. If the city department of purchase bought 190 computers for $793.50 each and 208 computers for $839.90 each, the TOTAL price paid for these computers is 9.____
   A. $315,813.00 B. $325,464.20
   C. $334,279.20 D. $335,863.00

Questions 10-14.

DIRECTIONS: Questions 10 through 14 are to be answered SOLELY on the basis of the information given in the following paragraph.

Since discounts are in common use in the commercial world and apply to purchases made by government agencies as well as business firms, it is essential that individuals in both public and private employment who prepare bills, check invoices, prepare payment vouchers, or write checks to pay bills have an understanding of the terms used. These include cash or time discount, trade discount, and disconnect series. A cash or time discount offers a reduction in price to the buyer for the prompt payment of the bill and is usually expressed as a percentage with a time requirement, stated in days, within which the bill must be paid in order to earn the discount. An example would be 3/10, meaning a 3% discount may be applied to the bill if the payment is forwarded to the vendor within ten days. On an invoice, the cash discount terms are usually followed by the net terms, which is the time in days allowed for ordinary payment of the bill. Thus, 3/10, Net 30 means that full payment is expected in thirty days if the cash discount of 3% is not taken for having paid the bill within ten days. When the expression Terms Net Cash is listed on a bill, it means that no deduction for early payment is allowed. A trade discount is normally applied to list prices by a manufacturer to show the actual price to retailers so that they may know their cost and determine markups that will allow them to operate competitively and at a profit. A trade discount is applied by the seller to the list price and is independent of a cash or time discount. Discounts may also be used by manufacturers to adjust prices charged to retailers without changing list prices. This is usually done by series discounting and is expressed as a series of percentages. To compute a series discount, such as 40%, 20%, 10%, first apply the 40% discount to the list price, then apply the 20% discount to the remainder, and finally apply the 10% discount to the second remainder.

10. According to the above passage, trade discounts are 10.____
   A. applied by the buyer B. independent of cash discounts
   C. restricted to cash sales D. used to secure rapid payment of bills

11. According to the above passage, if the sales terms 5/10, Net 60 appear on a bill in the amount of $100 dated December 5, 2016 and the buyer submits his payment on December 15, 2016, his PROPER payment should be 11.____
   A. $60 B. $90 C. $95 D. $100

12. According to the above passage, if a manufacturer gives a trade discount of 40% for an item with a list price of $250 and the terms are Net Cash, the price a retail merchant is required to pay for this item is 12.____
    A. $250 B. $210 C. $150 D. $100

13. According to the above passage, a series discount of 25%, 20%, 10% applied to a list price of $200 results in an ACTUAL price to the buyer of 13.____
    A. $88 B. $90 C. $108 D. $110

14. According to the above passage, if a manufacturer gives a trade discount of 50% and the terms are 6/10, Net 30, the cost to a retail merchant of an item with a list price of $500 and for which he takes the time discount is 14.____
    A. $220 B. $235 C. $240 D. $250

Questions 15-22.

DIRECTIONS: Questions 15 through 22 each show in Column I the information written on five cards (lettered j, k, l, m, n) which have to be filed. You are to choose the option (lettered A, B, C, or D) in Column II which BEST represents the proper order of filing according to the information, rules, and sample question given below.

A file card record is kept of the work assignments for all the employees in a certain bureau. On each card is the employee's name, the date of work assignment, and the work assignment code number. The cards are to be filed according to the following rules:

FIRST: File in alphabetical order according to employee's name.

SECOND: When two or more cards have the same employee's name, file according to the assignment date, beginning with the earliest date.

THIRD: When two or more cards have the same employee's name and the same date, file according to the work assignment number beginning with the lowest number.

Column II shows the cards arranged in four different orders. Pick the option (A, B, C, or D) in Column II which shows the correct arrangement of the cards according to th above filing rules.

SAMPLE QUESTION

Column I	Column II
j. Cluney 4/8/02 (486503)	A. k, l, m, j, n
k. Roster 5/10/01 (246611)	B. k, n, j, l, m
l. Altool 10/15/02 (711433)	C. l, k, j, m, n
m. Cluney 12/18/02 (527610)	D. l, n, j, m, k
n. Cluney 4/8/02 (486500)	

The correct way to file the cards is:
- l. Altool 10/15/02 (71143)
- n. Cluney 4/8/02 (486500)
- j. Cluney 4/8/02 (486503)
- m. Cluney 12/18/02 (527610)
- k. Roster 5/10/01 (246611)

The correct filing order is shown by the letters l, n, j, m, k. The answer to the sample question is the letter D, which appears in front of the letters l, n, j, m, k in Column II.

COLUMN I	COLUMN II	
15. j. Smith 3/19/03 (662118)	A. j, m, l, n, k	15.____
k. Turner 4/16/99 (481349)	B. j, l, n, m, k	
l. Terman 3/20/02 (210229)	C. k, n, m, l, j	
m. Smyth 3/20/02 (481359)	D. j, n, k, l, m	
n. Terry 5/11/01 (672128)		
16. j. Ross 5/29/02 (396118)	A. l, m, k, n, j	16.____
k. Rosner 5/29/02 (439281)	B. m, l, k, n, j	
l. Rose 7/19/02 (723456)	C. l, m, k, j, n	
m. Rosen 5/29/03 (829692)	D. m, l, j, n, k	
n. Ross 5/29/02 (399118)		
17. j. Sherd 10/12/99 (552368)	A. n, m, k, j, l	17.____
k. Snyder 11/12/99 (539286)	B. j, m, l, k, n	
l. Shindler 10/13/98 (426798)	C. m, k, n, j. l	
m. Scherld 10/12/99 (552386)	D. m, n, j, l, k	
n. Schneider 11/12/99 (798213)		
18. j. Carter 1/16/02 (489636)	A. k, n, j, l, m	18.____
k. Carson 2/16/01 (392671)	B. n, k, m, l, j	
l. Carter 1/16/01 (486936)	C. n, k, l, j, m	
m. Carton 3/15/00 (489639)	D. k, n, l, j, m	
n. Carson 2/16/01 (392617)		
19. j. Thomas 3/18/99 (763182)	A. m, l, j, k, n	19.____
k. Tompkins 3/19/00 (928439)	B. j, m, l, k, n	
l. Thomson 3/21/00 (763812)	C. j, l, n, m, k	
m. Thompson 3/18/99 (924893)	D. l, m, j, n, k	
n. Tompson 3/19/99 (928793)		
20. j. Breit 8/10/03 (345612)	A. m, j, n, k, l	20.____
k. Briet 5/21/00 (837543)	B. n, m, j, k, l	
l. Bright 9/18/99 (931827)	C. m, j, k, l, n	
m. Breit 3/7/98 (553984)	D. j, m, k, l, n	
n. Brent 6/14/04 (682731)		

COLUMN I	COLUMN II	
21. j. Roberts 10/19/02 (581932)	A. n, k, l, m, j	21.____
k. Rogers 8/9/00 (638763)	B. n, k, l, j, m	
l. Rogers 7/15/97 (105689)	C. k, n, l, m, j	
m. Robin 3/8/92 (287915)	D. j, m, k, n, l	
n. Rogers 4/2/04 (736921)		
22. j. Hebert 4/28/02 (719468)	A. n, k, j, m, l	22.____
k. Herbert 5/8/01 (938432)	B. j, l, n, k, m	
l. Helbert 9/23/04 (832912)	C. l, j, k, n, m	
m. Herbst 7/10/03 (648599)	D. l, j, n, k, m	
n. Herbert 5/8/01 (487627)		

23. In order to pay its employees, the Convex Company obtained bills and coins in the following denominations: 23.____

Denomination	$20	$10	$5	$1	$.50	$.25	$.10	$.05	$.01
Number	317	122	38	73	69	47	39	25	36

What was the TOTAL amount of cash obtained?
A. $7,874.76 B. $7,878.00 C. $7,889.25 D. $7,924.35

24. H. Partridge receives a weekly gross salary (before deductions) of $596.25. Through weekly payroll deductions of $19.77, he is paying back a load he took from his pension fund. 24.____
If other fixed weekly deductions amount to $184.14, how much pay would Mr. Partridge take home over a period of 33 weeks?
A. $11,446.92 B. $12,375.69 C. $12,947.22 D. $19,676.25

25. Mr. Robertson is a city employee enrolled in a city retirement system. He has taken out a loan from the retirement fund and is paying it back at the rate of $14.90 every two weeks. 25.____
In eighteen weeks, how much money will he have paid back on the loan?
A. $268.20 B. $152.80 C. $124.10 D. $67.05

26. In 2015, the Iridor Book Company had the following expenses: rent, $6,500; overhead, $52,585; inventory, $35,700; and miscellaneous, $1,275. 26.____
If all of these expenses went up 18% in 2016, what would they TOTAL in 2016?
A. $17,290.80 B. $78,768.20 C. $96,060.00 D. $113,350.80

27. Ms. Ranier had a gross salary of $355.36, paid once every week. 27.____
If the deductions from each paycheck are $62.72, $25.13, $6.29, and $1,27, how much money would Ms. Ranier take home in four weeks?
A. $1,039.80 B. $1,421.44 C. $2,079.60 D. $2,842.88

28. Mr. Martin had a net income of $19,100 for the year. 28.____
If he spent 34% on rent and household expenses, 3% on house furnishings, 25% on clothes, and 36% on food, how much was left for savings and other expenses?
A. $196.00 B. $382.00 C. $649.40 D. $1,960.00

29. Mr. Elsberg can pay back a loan of $1,800 from the city employees' retirement system if he pays back $36.69 every two weeks for two full years. 29.____
At the end of the two years, how much more than the original $1,800 he borrowed will Mr. Elsberg have paid back?
A. $53.94 B. $107.88 C. $190.79 D. $214.76

30. Mrs. Nusbaum is a city employee, receiving a gross salary (salary before deductions) of $31,200. Every two weeks, the following deductions are taken out of her salary: Federal Income Tax, $243.96; FICA, $66.39; State Tax, $44.58; City Tax, $20.91; Health Insurance, $4.71. 30.____
If Mrs. Nusbaum's salary and deductions remained the same for a full calendar year, what would her NET salary (gross salary less deductions) be in that year?
A. $9,894.30 B. $21,305.70 C. $28,118.25 D. $30,819.45

KEY (CORRECT ANSWERS)

1.	C	11.	C	21.	D
2.	A	12.	C	22.	B
3.	D	13.	C	33.	A
4.	C	14.	B	24.	C
5.	D	15.	A	25.	C
6.	A	16.	C	26.	D
7.	A	17.	D	27.	A
8.	B	18.	C	28.	B
9.	B	19.	B	29.	B
10.	B	20.	A	30.	B

EXAMINATION SECTION
TEST 1

DIRECTIONS: Each question or incomplete statement is followed by several suggested answers or completions. Select the one that BEST answers the question or completes the statement. *PRINT THE LETTER OF THE CORRECT ANSWER IN THE SPACE AT THE RIGHT.*

Questions 1-7.

DIRECTIONS: Questions 1 through 7 are to be answered on the basis of the following income statement.

Laura Lee's Bridal Shop
Income Statement
For the Year Ended December 31, 2018

Revenue:		
New & Used Bridal Gowns & Accessories		$55,000
Expenses:		
Advertisement Expense	$ 2,000	
Salaries Expense	12,000	
Dry cleaning & Alterations	10,000	
Utilities	1,500	
Total Expenses		25,500
Net Income		$29,500

1. What is the period of time covered by this income statement? 1.____

   A. January-December 2017
   B. December 2018
   C. January 2017-December 2018
   D. January-December 2018

2. What is the source of the revenue? 2.____

   A. New and used bridal gowns, advertisements, salaries, dry cleaning, and utilities
   B. Advertisements, salaries, dry cleaning, alterations, and utilities
   C. New and used bridal gowns and accessories
   D. Net income

3. What is the total revenue? 3.____

   A. $25,500 B. $55,000 C. $29,500 D. $79,500

4. Which of the following are expenses? 4.____

   A. Salaries
   B. New and used bridal gowns and accessories
   C. Revenue
   D. New and used bridal gowns, advertisements, and dry cleaning

5. What are the total expenses? 5.____

   A. $55,000 B. $29,500 C. $79,500 D. $25,500

6. There is a resulting net income because 6.____

   A. total revenue and total expenses are combined
   B. net income is greater than total revenue
   C. the total revenue is greater than total expenses
   D. the total revenue is less than total expenses

7. Is this statement an interim statement? 7.____

   A. *Yes*, because it covers an entire accounting period
   B. *No*, because it covers an entire accounting period
   C. *Yes*, because it covers a period of less than a year
   D. *No*, because it covers a period of more than a year

8. What is the name of the accounting report that may show either a net profit or a net loss for an accounting period? 8.____

   A. Income statement
   B. Balance sheet
   C. Statement of capital
   D. Classified balance sheet

9. What are the two main parts of the body of the income statement? 9.____

   A. Cash and Capital
   B. Revenue and Expenses
   C. Liabilities and Capital
   D. Assets and Notes Payable

10. If total revenue exceeds total expenses for an accounting period, what is the difference called? 10.____

    A. Gross income
    B. Total liabilities
    C. Total assets
    D. Net income

11. In the body of a balance sheet, what are the three sections called? 11.____

    A. Assets and liabilities
    B. Cash, liabilities, and revenue
    C. Assets, liabilities, and capital
    D. Revenue, assets, and capital

12. What business record shows the results of the proprietor's borrowing assets from the business, usually in anticipation of profits? 12.____

    A. Proprietor's withdrawals
    B. Accounts payable
    C. Liabilities and Capital
    D. Total liabilities

Questions 13-24.

DIRECTIONS: For each transaction given for Mona's Magic Moments Hair Salon in Questions 13 through 24, identify which journal the transaction should be recorded in.

13. April 1: Mona, the owner, paid the month's rent - $600.00; check no. 356. 13.____

    A. General
    B. Cash disbursements
    C. Purchases
    D. Sales

14. April 6: the salon purchased $300.00 worth of styling products on account from Pomme de Terre Company. 14.____

A. Cash disbursements B. General
C. Sales D. Purchases

15. April 8: sold $100.00 worth of hair products on account to Mrs. Angela Bray. 15.____

A. Sales B. Purchases
C. Cash disbursements D. General

16. April 11: the owner, Mona Ramen, withdrew $80.00 of styling products for personal use. 16.____

A. Sales B. Cash receipts
C. General D. Cash disbursements

17. April 13: paid Pomme de Terre Company $300.00 on account; check 357. 17.____

A. Purchases B. Cash disbursements
C. Cash receipts D. General

18. April 15: cash sales to date were $4,607.00. 18.____

A. Cash disbursements B. Purchases
C. Sales D. General

19. April 17: issued credit slip #17 to Mrs. Angela Bray for $25.00 for merchandise returned. 19.____

A. Cash disbursements B. Cash receipts
C. Sales D. General

20. April 19: paid electric bill for $250.00; check no. 358. 20.____

A. Cash disbursements B. Purchases
C. General D. Cash receipts

21. April 21: received $75.00 from Mrs. Angela Bray for balance due on account. 21.____

A. Sales B. Cash disbursements
C. Cash receipts D. Purchases

22. April 23: sold $88.00 of hair products on account to Ms. Tania Alioto. 22.____

A. Purchases B. Sales
C. Cash disbursements D. Cash receipts

23. April 27: purchased $500.00 of equipment from Salon Stylings Merchandisers on account. 23.____

A. Cash disbursements B. Sales
C. General D. Purchases

24. April 30: cash sales to date were $5023.00. 24.____

A. Purchases B. Sales
C. Cash receipts D. General

Questions 25-30.

DIRECTIONS: Questions 25 through 30 are to be answered on the basis of the following ledger for a barbecue take-out restaurant owned and operated by Ruby Joiner.

Cash	
450	150
212	125
328	440
172	125
250	70
275	150
325	50

Accounts Receivable	
360	170
250	100
165	120
100	60

Delivery Equipment	
5,000	
4,000	
3,000	

Supplies	
40	
65	
30	
25	

Ruby Joiner, Capital	
	8,200
	2,000
	2,097

Accounts Payable	
10	600
15	300
	200

Ruby Joiner, Drawing	
225	
175	
200	

Advertising Expense	
40	
45	

Delivery Income	
	400
	350
	250
	100

Trucking Expense	
100	
50	

Telephone Expense	
80	
40	
20	

25. What is the balance on the Cash account shown above? 25.____

A. 2,012.00 B. 1,110.00 C. 3,122.00 D. 902.00

26. What is the balance on the Accounts receivable account shown above? 26.____

A. 425.00 B. 875.00 C. 450.00 D. 1315.00

27. What is the balance on the Accounts payable account shown above? 27.____

A. 1100.00 B. 1075.00 C. 25.00 D. 1125.00

28. Which of the above accounts has a balance of 1100.00? 28.____

A. Accounts payable
B. Delivery Income
C. Cash
D. Delivery equipment

29. Which of the above accounts has a balance of 12,000.00? 29.____

A. Ruby Joiner, Capital
B. Cash and Accounts receivable combined
C. Delivery equipment
D. None of the accounts

30. If you made a balance sheet out of the information listed above, Ruby Joiner's total assets would be 30.____

A. 14,472.00 B. 12,297.00 C. 13,392.00 D. 13,487.00

Questions 31-34.

DIRECTIONS: Questions 31 through 34 are to be answered on the basis of the following information, to be included on a checking deposit ticket.

Five $20 bills; 11 $10 bills; 6 $5 bills; 47 $1 bills; 200 half dollars; 120 quarters; 112 dimes; 320 nickels; 67 pennies. Second National Bank (73-124) check of 152.34; Bank of the Midwest (13-298) check of 68.37; Great National Bank (32-165) check of 185.06.

31. What is the TOTAL currency for this deposit? 31.____

A. $387 B. $287 C. $444.87 D. $157.87

32. What is the TOTAL coin for this deposit? 32.____

A. $387 B. $287 C. $444.87 D. $157.87

33. What is the check total for this deposit? 33.____

A. $692.77 B. $406 C. $405.77 D. $850.64

34. What is the TOTAL deposit? 34.____

A. $444.87 B. $692.77 C. $851 D. $850.64

Questions 35-37.

DIRECTIONS: Questions 35 through 37 are to be answered on the basis of the following petty cash journal.

Date	Receipt No.	To Whom Paid	For What	Acct.#	Amount
10/2	1	Anna Jones - Mail	Postage	548	13.50
10/2	2	Jim Collins	Messenger	525	5.75
10/4	3	Anna Jones - Mail	Postage	548	13.50
10/5	4	Lucky Stores	Coffee	515	7.34
10/6	5	Tom Allen	Lunch w/customer	525	11.38

35. What is the TOTAL disbursement from this fund for the time period 10/1 through 10/6? 35.____

A. $51.47 B. $40.09 C. $61.47 D. $26.59

36. How much money was disbursed to Account #548 during the time period 10/1-10/16? 36.____

A. $51.47 B. $26 C. $27 D. $34.34

37. If the fund began the month with a total of $100.00, what amount was left in the fund at the end of business on 10/5? 37.____

A. $48.53 B. $59.91 C. $51.47 D. $40.09

Questions 38-40.

DIRECTIONS: Questions 38 through 40 are to be answered on the basis of the following information.

A promissory note dated December 1, 2018, bearing interest at a rate of 12% and due in 90 days, is sent to a creditor. The face value of the note is $900.

38. What is the due date of the promissory note? 38.____

A. January 15, 2019   B. March 1, 2019
C. February 1, 2019   D. December 31, 2018

39. What is the TOTAL interest that will be earned on the note? 39.____

A. $27   B. $270   C. $108   D. $10.80

40. What interest will be earned on the note for the old accounting period (December 1-31)? 40.____

A. $90   B. $36   C. $9   D. $3.60

KEY (CORRECT ANSWERS)

1. D	11. C	21. C	31. B
2. C	12. A	22. B	32. D
3. B	13. B	23. D	33. C
4. A	14. D	24. B	34. D
5. D	15. A	25. D	35. A
6. C	16. C	26. A	36. C
7. B	17. B	27. B	37. B
8. A	18. C	28. B	38. B
9. B	19. D	29. C	39. A
10. D	20. A	30. D	40. C

TEST 2

DIRECTIONS: Each question or incomplete statement is followed by several suggested answers or completions. Select the one that BEST answers the question or completes the statement. *PRINT THE LETTER OF THE CORRECT ANSWER IN THE SPACE AT THE RIGHT.*

Questions 1-4.

DIRECTIONS: Questions 1 through 4 are to be answered on the basis of the following information, to be included in a deposit slip.

14 twenty dollar bills	63 quarters
52 ten dollar bills	22 dimes
12 five dollar bills	44 nickels
43 one dollar bills	70 pennies

Checks: $236.34 and $129.72

1. What is the TOTAL amount of currency for this deposit? 1.____

   A. $923.85 B. $1269.06 C. $903.00 D. $1299.91

2. What is the TOTAL amount of coin for this deposit? 2.____

   A. $20.85 B. $923.85 C. $903.00 D. $1299.91

3. What is the TOTAL amount of check for this deposit? 3.____

   A. $20.85 B. $366.06 C. $1299.91 D. $903.00

4. What is the TOTAL deposit for this slip? 4.____

   A. $1269.06 B. $903.00 C. $923.85 D. $1289.91

Questions 5-7.

DIRECTIONS: Questions 5 through 7 are to be answered on the basis of the following information.

Angela Martinez's last check stub balance was $675.50. Her bank statement balance dated April 30 was $652.00. A $250 deposit was in transit on that date. Outstanding checks were as follows: No. 127, $65.00; No. 129, $203.50; No. 130, $50.00. The bank service charge for the month was $5.00.

5. What was Angela Martinez's available checkbook balance on April 30? 5.____

   A. $652.00 B. $338.50 C. $583.50 D. $675.50

6. In order to reconcile her checkbook balance with her bank statement balance, what must Angela Martinez do? 6.____

   A. Add her checkbook balance to the balance on her bank statement
   B. Subtract her checkbook balance from the balance on her bank statement

C. Ignore her checkbook balance and adopt the balance on her bank statement
D. Adjust the checkbook balance by adding deposits and debiting outstanding checks and charges

7. The check stub balance referred to in the problem refers to the 7.____

A. last check Angela Martinez recorded in her checkbook
B. amount of money left in Angela Martinez's account according to her own calculations based on the checks, charges, and deposits she has written and recorded
C. amount of money left in Angela Martinez's account according to the bank's calculations based on the checks, charges, and deposits posted to her account
D. number of checks left in her checkbook

Questions 8-9.

DIRECTIONS: Questions 8 and 9 are to be answered on the basis of the following information.

Tu Nguyen, an interior designer, received his June bank statement on July 2. The balance was $622.66. His last check stub balance was $700. On comparing the two, he noticed that a deposit of $275 made on June 30 was not included on the statement; also, a bank service charge of $4 was deducted. Outstanding checks were as follows: No. 331, $97.50; No. 332, $207; No. 335, $25.40; and No. 336, $68.97.

8. What is Nguyen's CORRECT available bank balance? 8.____

A. $494.79 B. $897.66 C. $700.00 D. $219.79

9. The bank statement balance referred to in the problem refers to the 9.____

A. last check Tu Nguyen recorded in his checkbook
B. last check presented for payment to Tu Nguyen's account
C. amount of money left in Tu Nguyen's account according to the bank's calculations based on the checks, charges, and deposits posted to his account
D. amount of money left in Tu Nguyen's account based on his own calculations of the checks, charges, and deposits he has written and recorded

10. What of the following endorsements would be an example of a simple Endorsement in Blank? 10.____

A. Pay to the Order of Joanie Anderson
B. Joanie Anderson
C. For deposit only; Acct. No. 12345; Joanie Anderson
D. Without Recourse; Joanie Anderson

11. Which of the following endorsements would limit the further purpose or use of the endorsed check? 11.____

A. Pay to the Order of Joanie Anderson
B. Joanie Anderson
C. For deposit only; Acct. No. 12345; Joanie Anderson,
D. Without Recourse; Joanie Anderson

12. Which of the following endorsements would protect the endorser from legal responsibility for payment, should the drawer have insufficient funds to honor his/her own check? 12.____

A. Pay to the Order of Joanie Anderson
B. Joanie Anderson
C. For deposit only; Acct. No. 12345; Joanie Anderson
D. Without Recourse; Joanie Anderson

Questions 13-24.

DIRECTIONS: Questions 13 - 24 are to be answered on the basis of the following ledger accounts for Wheelsmith Organic Farms.

Wheelsmith Organic Farms
Ledger Accounts

Cash	
Jan. 1 4,000	

Accounts Payable	
	Jan. 1 2,000

Service Supplies	
Jan. 1 2,000	

Shelley Wheelsmith, Capital	
	Jan. 1 11,000

Machinery	
Jan. 1 7,000	

13. Transaction #1: On January 5, Shelley Wheelsmith, the proprietor, received cash amounting to $5,000 as a result of returning machinery that had recently been purchased. What account(s) should this transaction be posted to? 13.____

A. Cash
B. Cash and Machinery
C. Machinery
D. Cash, Machinery, and Service Supplies

14. Transaction #2: On January 8, Shelley Wheelsmith, the proprietor, sent out a check for $600 in partial payment of the accounts payable. What account(s) should this transaction be posted to? 14.____

A. Accounts Payable
B. Accounts Payable and Cash
C. Accounts Payable and Capital
D. Cash

15. Transaction #3: On January 14, Shelley Wheelsmith, proprietor, made an additional investment in the business by contributing machinery valued at $1,500. What account(s) should this transaction be posted to? 15.____

A. Machinery
B. Machinery and Capital
C. Capital
D. Machinery and Cash

16. Transaction #4: On January 26, Shelley Wheelsmith, proprietor, purchased additional service supplies for $200. She agreed to pay the obligation in 30 days. What account(s) should this transaction be posted to? 16.____

A. Accounts Payable and Liabilities
B. Service supplies
C. Accounts Payable
D. Accounts Payable and Service supplies

17. Transaction #5: On January 31, Shelley Wheelsmith, proprietor, purchased service supplies paying cash of $50. What account(s) should this transaction be posted to? 17.____

A. Service supplies
B. Service supplies and Accounts Payable
C. Cash and Service supplies
D. Cash

18. What is the balance in the Cash account after all of these transactions are posted? 18.____

A. $9,000 B. $1,000 C. $5,000 D. $8,350

19. What is the balance in the Machinery account after all of these transactions are posted? 19.____

A. $7,000 B. $5,000 C. $3,500 D. $13,500

20. What is the balance in the Accounts Payable account after all of these transactions are posted? 20.____

A. $800 B. $600 C. $2,600 D. $1,600

21. What is the balance in the Capital account after all of these transactions are posted? 21.____

A. $12,500 B. $800 C. $11,600 D. $10,400

22. What is the balance in the Service supplies account after all of these transactions are posted? 22.____

A. $2,000 B. $2,250 C. $750 D. $2,200

23. What are the total assets of Wheelsmith Organic Farms after these transactions have been posted? 23.____

A. $10,600 B. $11,850 C. $14,100 D. $10,750

24. What are the total liabilities and capital for Wheelsmith Organic Farms after these transactions have been posted? 24.____

A. $14,100 B. $12,500 C. $11,850 D. $10,600

Questions 25-28.

DIRECTIONS: Questions 25 through 28 are to be answered on the basis of the following information.

At the end of an accounting period, Andy's Framing Gallery recorded the following information: Sales, $125,225; Merchandise Inventory, December 31, $95,325; Purchases Returns and Allowances, $3,500; Merchandise Inventory, January 1, $98,725; Freight on Purchases, $2,500; Purchases, $120,000.

25. What are the net purchases for Andy's Framing Gallery during the accounting period? 25.____

A. $120,000 B. $119,000 C. $3,500 D. $122,500

26. What is the cost of goods available for sale? 26.____

A. $119,000 B. $98,725 C. $95,325 D. $217,725

27. What is the total cost of goods sold for this accounting period? 27.____

A. $217,725 B. $95,325 C. $122,400 D. $125,225

28. What is the gross profit on sales for this accounting period? 28.____

A. $2825 B. $2500 C. $125,225 D. $122,400

Questions 29-40.

DIRECTIONS: Questions 29 through 40 are to be answered on the basis of the following information.

The Joie de Vivre Co. received the promissory notes listed below during the last quarter of its calendar year:

	Date	Face Amount	Terms	Interest Rate	Date Discounted	Discount Rate
(1)	10/8	$3,600	30 days	-	10/18	9%
(2)	9/22	$8,000	60 days	6%	10/1	7%
(3)	11/15	$3,000	90 days	7%	11/20	8%

29. What is the due date for the first note? 29.____

A. 12/31 B. 11/7 C. 12/7 D. 10/31

30. What interest will be due when the first note matures? 30.____

A. $3 B. $3,600 C. $30 D. $0

31. What is the maturity value of the first note? 31.____

A. $3,600 B. $3,630 C. $0 D. $3,603

32. What is the discount period for the first note? 32.____

A. One fiscal year B. 10 days
C. 20 days D. One month

33. What is the due date for the second note? 33.____

A. 12/21 B. 11/21 C. 10/21 D. 1/21

34. What interest will be due when the second note matures? 34.____

A. $60 B. $800.00 C. $8.00 D. $80.00

35. What is the maturity value of the second note? 35.____

A. $8,000 B. $8,080 C. $8,800 D. $8,008

36. What is the discount period for the second note? 36.____

A. 51 days B. 10 days C. 360 days D. 60 days

37. What is the due date for the third note? 37.____

A. 1/14 B. 12/15 C. 12/31 D. 2/13

38. What interest will be due when the third note matures? 38.____

A. $5.25 B. $52.50 C. $525 D. $90

39. What is the maturity value of the third note? 39.____

A. $3525 B. $3005.25 C. $3052.50 D. $3090

40. What is the discount period for the third note? 40.____

A. 60 days B. 85 days C. 5 days D. 90 days

KEY (CORRECT ANSWERS)

1.	C	11.	C	21.	A	31.	A
2.	A	12.	D	22.	B	32.	C
3.	B	13.	B	23.	C	33.	B
4.	D	14.	B	24.	A	34.	D
5.	C	15.	B	25.	B	35.	B
6.	D	16.	D	26.	D	36.	A
7.	B	17.	C	27.	C	37.	D
8.	A	18.	D	28.	A	38.	B
9.	C	19.	C	29.	B	39.	C
10.	B	20.	D	30.	D	40.	B

TEST 3

DIRECTIONS: Each question or incomplete statement is followed by several suggested answers or completions. Select the one that BEST answers the question or completes the statement. *PRINT THE LETTER OF THE CORRECT ANSWER IN THE SPACE AT THE RIGHT.*

Questions 1-8.

DIRECTIONS: Questions 1 through 8 are to be answered on the basis of the following Balance Sheet.

Laura Lee's Bridal Shop
Balance Sheet
December 31, 2018

Assets		
Cash	$14,000	
Accounts Receivable	3,000	
Bridal Accessories	10,000	
Gowns and Other Inventory	30,000	
Total Assets		$57,000
Liabilities and Capital		
Accounts Payable	$ 4,000	
Notes Payable	28,000	
Total Liabilities		$32,000
Laura Lee, Capital		25,000
Total Liabilities and Capital		$57,000

1. When was the balance sheet prepared? 1.____

    A. January 2019
    B. December 31, 2018
    C. After the close of the 2018 fiscal year
    D. December 1, 2018

2. How does the date on this balance sheet differ from the date on the statement of capital or income statement? 2.____

    A. It doesn't differ. The dates for each statement signify the same time period.
    B. The date on a balance sheet represents the period during which any changes indicated on the statement took place, whereas the other financial statements represent the moment in time when the statement was prepared.
    C. The date on a balance sheet represents the moment in time when the statement was prepared, whereas the other financial statements represent the period during which any changes indicated on the statement took place.
    D. The date on a balance sheet indicates an entire year, whereas the dates on the other statements indicate a single month.

3. Can Laura Lee purchase more bridal gowns for the business paying cash of $16,000? 3.____

    A. *No*, because the business has only $14,000 cash available
    B. *Yes*, because the business has $57,000 cash available
    C. *Yes*, because the business has $57,000 available in assets
    D. *No*, because the business has $57,000 in liabilities

4. What is the owner's equity of Laura Lee's Bridal Shop? Since total equity consists of total ______, total equity is ______. 4.____

   A. assets minus total liabilities and proprietor's capital; $0
   B. assets minus total liabilities; $25,000
   C. assets; $57,000
   D. liabilities and proprietor's capital; $57,000

5. What is the TOTAL amount of Laura Lee's claim against the total assets of the business? 5.____

   A. $57,000 B. $25,000 C. $0 D. $39,000

6. What is the amount of the creditors' claims against the assets of the business? 6.____

   A. $4,000 B. $57,000 C. $32,000 D. $28,000

7. What is the net income for the period? 7.____

   A. $57,000
   B. $0
   C. $25,000
   D. This information cannot be obtained from the balance sheet

8. What was the value of Laura Lee's ownership in this business on January 1, 2004? 8.____

   A. $25,000
   B. $57,000
   C. $14,000
   D. This information cannot be obtained from the balance sheet

Questions 9-21.

DIRECTIONS: Each of the transactions described in Questions 9 through 21 occurred within an accounting period. For each question, indicate which of the four journals the transaction would be recorded in.

9. Sale of goods on account 9.____

   A. Cash receipts B. Cash payments
   C. General D. Sales

10. Cash payment of a promissory note 10.____

   A. Cash payments B. Cash receipts
   C. Sales D. General

11. Received a credit memo from a creditor 11.____

   A. Purchases B. General
   C. Sales D. Cash payments

12. Sale of merchandise for cash 12.____

   A. Purchases B. General
   C. Cash receipts D. Cash payments

13. Received a check from a customer in partial payment of an oral agreement 13.____

A. Purchases
B. Sales
C. General
D. Cash receipts

14. Issued a credit memo to a customer 14.____

A. Purchases
B. General
C. Cash payments
D. Sales

15. Received a promissory note in place of an oral agreement from a customer 15.____

A. General
B. Cash payments
C. Cash receipts
D. Sales

16. Paid monthly rent 16.____

A. General
B. Purchases
C. Cash payments
D. Cash receipts

17. Sale of a service on credit 17.____

A. Cash receipts
B. General
C. Purchases
D. Sales

18. Purchase of office furniture on credit 18.____

A. General
B. Purchases
C. Cash payments
D. Cash receipts

19. Purchased merchandise for cash 19.____

A. Cash payments
B. Cash receipts
C. Sales
D. General

20. Cash refund to a customer 20.____

A. Cash receipts
B. Sales
C. General
D. Cash payments

21. Purchases made on credit 21.____

A. Purchases
B. Sales
C. Cash receipts
D. General

Questions 22-26.

DIRECTIONS: Questions 22 through 26 are to be answered on the basis of the following inventory, purchased by International Soap and Candle Traders, Inc.

700 units at $4.50, 320 units at $3.75, 550 units at $2.75, and 475 units at $1.90

22. Calculate the total price of the units that cost $4.50. 22.____

A. $315 B. $31,500 C. $3,150 D. $2,800

23. Calculate the total price of the units that cost $3.75. 23.____

A. $2062.50 B. $12,000 C. $120 D. $1,200

24. Calculate the total price of the units that cost $2.75. 24.____

A. $1,512.50 B. $15,125 C. $151.25 D. $550

25. Calculate the total price of the units that cost $1.90. 25.____

A. $90.25 B. $9025 C. $902.50 D. $475

26. Calculate the average cost per unit. 26.____

A. $27 B. $33.10 C. $0.30 D. $3.31

27. The interest on a promissory note is recorded at which of the following times? 27.____

A. When the debt is incurred
B. At the end of the accounting period
C. When the note is paid
D. At the beginning of each month

28. The interest on a promissory note begins accruing at which of the following times? 28.____

A. When the debt is incurred
B. At the end of the accounting period
C. When the note is paid
D. At the beginning of each month

29. The maturity value of an interest-bearing note is the 29.____

A. interest accrued on the note plus a service charge imposed by the lender
B. interest accrued on the note
C. face value of the note
D. principal of the note plus interest

30. A cash receipts journal is used to record the 30.____

A. number of cash sales a business makes
B. number of credit sales a business makes
C. collection of cash made by the business
D. expenditure of cash made by the business

31. Calculate the interest on a promissory note issued for $3,000 at an interest rate of 8%, due in 360 days. (Assume a banking year of 360 days.) 31.____

A. $300 B. $240 C. $60 D. $360

32. Calculate the total payment due for a promissory note issued for $1,000 at an interest rate of 10%, due in 90 days. (Assume a banking year of 360 days.) 32.____

A. $25 B. $1050 C. $1000 D. $1025

33. Calculate the total payment due for a promissory note issued for $5,000 at an interest rate of 6%, due in 60 days. (Assume a banking year of 360 days.) 33.____

A. $5,050 B. $50 C. $5,000 D. $5,300

34. Calculate the interest on a promissory note issued for $1,700 at an interest rate of 12%, due in 45 days. (Assume a banking year of 360 days.) 34.____

A. $204 B. $1725.50 C. $25.50 D. $1904

35. Calculate the interest on a promissory note issued for $600 at an interest rate of 9%, due in 90 days. (Assume a banking year of 360 days.) 35.____

A. $13.50 B. $135 C. $54 D. $540

KEY (CORRECT ANSWERS)

1. B	16. C
2. C	17. D
3. A	18. B
4. B	19. A
5. B	20. D
6. C	21. A
7. D	22. C
8. D	23. D
9. D	24. A
10. A	25. C
11. B	26. D
12. C	27. C
13. D	28. A
14. B	29. D
15. A	30. C

31. B
32. D
33. A
34. C
35. A

EXAMINATION SECTION

TEST 1

DIRECTIONS: Each question or incomplete statement is followed by several suggested answers or completions. Select the one that BEST answers the question or completes the statement. *PRINT THE LETTER OF THE CORRECT ANSWER IN THE SPACE AT THE RIGHT.*

Questions 1-20.

DIRECTIONS: Listed below in T accounts are the five MAJOR classifications of accounts. Consider carefully each of the following statements and indicate the change by writing the appropriate letter from the T accounts in the space at the right.

ASSETS		LIABILITIES		PROPRIETORSHIP		INCOME		EXPENSES	
A	B	C	D	E	F	G	H	I	J

Sample Question:
A decrease in cash
The CORRECT answer is B.

1. An increase in equipment 1.____

2. An increase in the proprietorship 2.____

3. An increase in office salaries 3.____

4. A decrease in accounts payable 4.____

5. An increase in merchandise inventory 5.____

6. A decrease in office equipment 6.____

7. A decrease in office supplies 7.____

8. An increase in the proprietor's drawing account 8.____

9. A withdrawal of capital by the proprietor 9.____

10. An increase in sales 10.____

11. An increase in salaries payable 11.____

12. An increase in the net profit for the period 12.____

13. An increase in the sales returns and allowances 13.____

14. A decrease in purchases 14.____

15. A decrease in the accounts receivable 15.____

16. An increase in the mortgage payable 16.____

17. An increase in delivery expense 17.____

18. An increase in notes payable 18.____

19. An increase in purchases returns and allowances 19.____

20. A decrease in delivery equipment 20.____

Questions 21-40.

DIRECTIONS: Indicate the title of the accounts to be debited and credited in journalizing, adjusting, and closing the transactions given below by writing in the space at the right the letters that correspond to the accounts listed at the right.

Sample Question:
Paid the rent for the month, $100

	Debit	Credit
Paid the rent for the month, $100	K	C

A. Accounts Payable
B. Accounts Receivable
C. Cash
D. Income & Expense Summary
E. Insurance
F. Insurance Expense
G. Merchandise Inventory
H. Office Supplies
I. Office Supplies Used
J. Purchases
K. Rent Expense
L. Salaries
M. Salaries Payable
N. Sales
O. C.M. Smith, Capital
P. C.M. Smith, Drawing

		Debit	Credit
21.	C.M. Smith invested $10,000 in the business	21.____	_____
22.	Purchased merchandise on account from A.D. Hall, $875	22.____	_____
23.	Sold merchandise on account to L.S. Brook, $500	23.____	_____
24.	Received $250 from cash sales	24.____	_____
25.	Purchased office supplies for cash, $90	25.____	_____
26.	Paid A.D. Hall $500 to apply on account	26.____	_____
27.	Paid insurance premium for the year, $360	27.____	_____
28.	Paid C.M. Smith $100 for personal use	28.____	_____
29.	Received $300 from L.S. Brooks, to apply on account	29.____	_____

30. Paid salaries for the month $500 — 30.____ ____

Adjusting Entries

31. The supplies used during the month were $60 — 31.____ ____

32. The salaries owed at the close of the month were $40 — 32.____ ____

33. The prepaid insurance expired was $30 — 33.____ ____

34. The beginning merchandise inventory was $1200 — 34.____ ____

35. The closing merchandise inventory was $750 — 35.____ ____

Closing Entries

36. The sales account has a balance of $4500 — 36.____ ____

37. The salaries for the month were $540 — 37.____ ____

38. The purchase account balance is $3600 — 38.____ ____

39. The office supplies used were $75 — 39.____ ____

40. The income and expense summary has a net profit of $350 — 40.____ ____

KEY (CORRECT ANSWERS)

					DEBIT	CREDIT		DEBIT	CREDIT
1.	A	11.	D	21.	C	O	31.	I	H
2.	F	12.	F	22.	J	A	32.	L	M
3.	I	13.	G	23.	B	N	33.	F	E
4.	C	14.	J	24.	C	N	34.	D	G
5.	A	15.	B	25.	H	C	35.	G	D
6.	B	16.	D	26.	A	C	36.	N	D
7.	B	17.	I	27.	E	C	37.	D	L
8.	E	18.	D	28.	P	C	38.	D	J
9.	E	19.	J	29.	C	B	39.	D	I
10.	H	20.	B	30.	L	C	40.	D	O

TEST 2

DIRECTIONS: Each question or incomplete statement is followed by several suggested answers or completions. Select the one that BEST answers the question or completes the statement. *PRINT THE LETTER OF THE CORRECT ANSWER IN THE SPACE AT THE RIGHT.*

Questions 1-16.

DIRECTIONS: Read each statement carefully. If you believe that the account should be debited, place a D for DEBIT in the space at the right. If you think it should be credited, place a C for CREDIT in the space at the right.

1. When sales are made for cash, the sales account is (debited or credited). 1.____

2. When sales are made on account, the customer's account is (debited or credited). 2.____

3. When merchandise is purchased for cash, the purchases account is (debited or credited). 3.____

4. The creditor's account is (debited or credited) when payment is made on account. 4.____

5. The sales account is (debited or credited) for the total of the amount column in the Sales Journal. 5.____

6. The cash account is (debited or credited) for the total of the cash column in the Cash Receipts Journal. 6.____

7. The purchases account is (debited or credited) for the total amount of the purchases column in the Purchases Journal. 7.____

8. The accounts receivable account is (debited or credited) for the total amount of the Sales Journal. 8.____

9. Each account in the Sales Journal is posted to the (debit or credit) of the customer's account. 9.____

10. The total of the accounts payable column in the Cash Payments Journal is posted to the (debit or credit) of the accounts payable account. 10.____

11. The total of the cash column in the Cash Payments Journal is posted to the (debit or credit) of the cash account. 11.____

12. Each account with an amount entered in the General column of the Cash Receipts Journal is (debited or credited). 12.____

13. When the proprietor invests additional cash in the business, the capital account is (debited or credited). 13.____

14. When merchandise is purchased on account, the purchases account is (debited or credited). 14.____

15. When sales salaries are unpaid at the close of the fiscal period, the salaries payable account is (debited or credited). 15.____

16. When equipment is purchased on account, the creditor's account is (debited or credited). 16.____

Questions 17-30.

DIRECTIONS: The following figures have been taken from Income Statements. Certain figures have been omitted and letters have been substituted. Determine the CORRECT amounts that should be recorded for each of the letters and write this amount in the space at the right. Each line across the page is a separate income statement.

Sales	Beginning Inventory	Purchases	Closing Inventory	Cost of Goods Sold	Gross Profit	Expenses	Net Profit	Net Loss
22,000	8,000	12,000	A	15,000	B	4,000	C	
D	E	60,000	30,000	40,000	10,000	F		2,000
3,500	1,000	2,500	500	G	500	H	100	
7,500	500	I	2,000	J	1,000	800	K	
30,000	L	25,000	5,000	28,000	M	2,500		N

17. A 17.____

18. B 18.____

19. C 19.____

20. D 20.____

21. E 21.____

22. F 22.____

23. G 23.____

24. H 24.____

25. I 25.____

26. J 26.____

27. K 27.____

28. L 28.____

29. M 29.____

30. N 30.____

KEY (CORRECT ANSWERS)

1.	C	11.	C	21.	10,000
2.	D	12.	C	22.	12,000
3.	D	13.	C	23.	3,000
4.	D	14.	D	24.	400
5.	C	15.	C	25.	8,000
6.	D	16.	C	26.	6,500
7.	D	17.	5,000	27.	200
8.	D	18.	7,000	28.	8,000
9.	D	19.	3,000	29.	2,000
10.	D	20.	50,000	30.	500

TEST 3

Questions 1-25

DIRECTIONS: Each of Questions 1 through 25 consists of a statement. You are to indicate whether the statement is TRUE (T) or FALSE (F). *PRINT THE LETTER OF THE CORRECT ANSWER IN THE SPACE AT THE RIGHT.*

1. One of the primary objectives of the proprietor of a business is to increase his proprietorship by earning a profit. 1.____

2. The length of time covered by the Income and Expense Statement is of no importance or significance. 2.____

3. The length of time covered by the Balance Sheet is of no importance or significance. 3.____

4. When a customer takes advantage of a cash discount, the amount of cash received is more than the amount of the invoice for which payment is received. 4.____

5. Posting of column totals from the Cash Receipts Journal to the General Ledger is done each day. 5.____

6. After the adjustments have been entered in their appropriate column in the worksheet, their equality is proved by adding the columns. 6.____

7. The amount of unsold merchandise is found by subtracting the merchandise sales from the merchandise purchased. 7.____

8. In the Income and Expense Statement, the sales minus the cost of goods sold equals the gross profit. 8.____

9. If the operating expenses exceed the gross profit, a net loss results. 9.____

10. Only asset, liability, and capital accounts appear in the post-closing trial balance. 10.____

11. The earning of a net profit by a business results in an increase in the net worth of the business. 11.____

12. If the assets of a business are less than the liabilities, the business is solvent. 12.____

13. Small business can use accounting and data processing machines to a better advantage than large businesses. 13.____

14. The adjusting entries can be prepared from the adjustment columns of the worksheet. 14.____

15. The amount of the supplies used during the fiscal period is credited to the supplies account at the close of the fiscal period. 15.____

16. If the credit side of the income and expense summary account is larger than the debit side, the difference is a net loss to the business. 16.____

17. The discount on sales is considered to be a part of the regular operating expenses of the business. 17.____

18. In writing off a customer's uncollectible amount, the allowance for bad debts in the General Ledger is credited. 18.____

19. The amount credited to the allowance for bad debts account is an estimated amount. 19.____

20. The allowance for depreciation account usually has a credit balance. 20.____

21. The time received for a fixed asset at the time it is replaced is always equal to its book value. 21.____

22. Prepaid expenses are sometimes called deferred credits to income. 22.____

23. Expenses that are incurred but not paid are termed accrued expenses. 23.____

24. Prepaid expenses may be shown on the balance sheet as a current asset. 24.____

25. Equipment is listed on the balance sheet as a fixed asset. 25.____

Questions 26-30.

DIRECTIONS: Questions 26 through 30 are to be answered by writing the CORRECT amount in the space at the right.

26. The office supplies account has a balance of $150 at the close of the fiscal period. The actual inventory of supplies is $60. What is the amount of supplies used during the period? 26.____

27. A company receives $490 in cash from a customer for the prompt payment of an invoice. Two percent was the discount. What was the original amount of the invoice? 27.____

28. The balance of the store supplies before adjustment is $400. The total cost of the store supplies on hand at the end of the period is $150. What is the amount of the adjusting entry? 28.____

29. What is the amount necessary to pay a $300 invoice, terms 3/10, 2/20, n/30, twelve days after date? 29.____

30. If equipment costing $1,500, with an estimated life of ten years, was purchased, what is the annual rate of depreciation? 30.____

KEY (CORRECT ANSWERS)

1.	T	11.	T	21.	F
2.	F	12.	F	22.	F
3.	T	13.	F	23.	T
4.	F	14.	T	24.	T
5.	F	15.	T	25.	T
6.	T	16.	F	26.	$90
7.	F	17.	F	27.	$500
8.	T	18.	F	28.	$250
9.	T	19.	T	29.	$294
10.	T	20.	T	30.	10%

TEST 4

DIRECTIONS: Each question or incomplete statement is followed by several suggested answers or completions. Select the one that BEST answers the question or completes the statement. *PRINT THE LETTER OF THE CORRECT ANSWER IN THE SPACE AT THE RIGHT.*

Questions 1-12.

DIRECTIONS: Each of Questions 1 through 12 consists of a statement. You are to indicate whether the statement is TRUE (T) or FALSE (F). *PRINT THE LETTER OF THE CORRECT ANSWER IN THE SPACE AT THE RIGHT.*

1. The supplies used during a fiscal period are shown on the balance sheet as a current asset. 1.____

2. If the assets and liabilities increase equally, the proprietorship also increases. 2.____

3. The Income and Expense Statement shows the results of business operations over a period of time. 3.____

4. An exchange of one asset for another asset of different value causes a change in the proprietorship. 4.____

5. The recording of allowance for depreciation actually results in writing down the asset values. 5.____

6. If the closing merchandise inventory is understated, the profit for the period will be understated. 6.____

7. If accrued salaries during a period are not recorded, the profit for the period will be overstated. 7.____

8. If sales returns are understated during a fiscal period, the profit for that period will be understated. 8.____

9. Unpaid salaries should be added to the salaries for the period before the profit for the period is figured. 9.____

10. When posting the Sales Journal, each item is posted separately to the accounts receivable controlling account in the General Ledger. 10.____

11. A business is said to be solvent when it has a net profit for the period. 11.____

12. Accrued income is income earned but not received during a fiscal period. 12.____

Questions 13-30.

DIRECTIONS: Below is a list of terms with an accompanying list of definitions or explanations. In the space at the right, put the letter of the term in Column II which BEST explains the definition or explanation in Column I.

COLUMN I

13. Entries needed to bring accounts up to date at the end of an accounting period 13.____
14. An entry in a book of original entry that has more than one debit or credit 14.____
15. An account used to summarize the income and expense data at the close of the fiscal period 15.____
16. An account with a balance that is partly a balance sheet amount and partly an income statement amount 16.____
17. Discount granted to a customer for early payment of his account 17.____
18. A journal designed for recording a particular type of transaction only 18.____
19. A ledger used for recording the details of a single account 19.____
20. An account in the general ledger that is supported by a subsidiary ledger 20.____
21. A list of individual account balances in a subsidiary ledger 21.____
22. Expense items bought and paid for, but not entirely consumed during the fiscal period 22.____
23. Expenses incurred but not paid during a fiscal period 23.____
24. The decrease in the value of a fixed asset due to wear and tear 24.____
25. The amount of unsold merchandise on hand 25.____

COLUMN II

A. Abstract
B. Accrued expenses
C. Adjusting entries
D. Allowance for bad debts
E. Book value
F. Cash discount
G. Compound entry
H. Controlling account
I. Current asset
J. Depreciation
K. Fixed asset
L. General ledger
M. Income & expense summary
N. Merchandise inventory
O. Mixed account
P. Petty cash
Q. Prepaid expenses
R. Retail method
S. Special journal
T. Straight-line method
U. Subsidiary ledger
V. Voucher

26. Assets of a more or less permanent nature used in the business 26.____

27. The amount of estimated uncollectible accounts receivable. 27.____

28. The most commonly used method of computing depreciation 28.____

29. The difference between the original cost of an asset and its valuation amount 29.____

30. A written authorization required for each expenditure 30.____

KEY (CORRECT ANSWERS)

1.	F	11.	F	21.	A
2.	F	12.	T	22.	Q
3.	T	13.	C	23.	B
4.	T	14.	G	24.	J
5.	F	15.	M	25.	N
6.	T	16.	O	26.	K
7.	T	17.	F	27.	D
8.	F	18.	S	28.	T
9.	T	19.	U	29.	E
10.	F	20.	H	30.	V

TEST 5

Questions 1-12.

DIRECTIONS: Questions 1 through 12 are to be answered by writing the CORRECT amount in the space at the right.

1. If the purchases for the month were $500, the beginning inventory was $1,500, the ending inventory was $1,000, and the gross profit was $2,000, what were the sales? 1.____

2. If the gross profit for the period was $750 and the net profit was $250, what was the amount of the expenses? 2.____

3. Determine the amount of the cost of goods sold if the purchases for the month were $10,000, the beginning inventory was $3,000, and the ending inventory was $5,000. 3.____

4. A typewriter was purchased for $300 with an estimated life of five years. What is the book value at the end of the third year? 4.____

5. A delivery truck costs $3,000. Its book value at the end of the third year was $2,100. What is the amount of depreciation each year? 5.____

6. The assets on a Balance Sheet are $7,500. The liabilities are $4,500. What is the capital? 6.____

7. A check was received for $242.50 in payment of a sale amounting to $250 less discount. What is the percent of discount allowed? 7.____

8. The capital at the close of the fiscal period was $10,000. The liabilities were $12,000. What are the TOTAL assets? 8.____

9. A note is dated March 1 and is due in 60 days. What is its due date? 9.____

10. A note is dated January 30. It is due in one month. What is its due date? 10.____

11. What is the interest on a note for $500 with interest at 6% for sixty days? 11.____

12. What is the interest on a note for $800 with interest at 6% for 45 days? 12.____

Questions 13-15

DIRECTIONS: Each of Questions 13 through 25 consists of a statement. You are to indicate whether the statement is TRUE (T) or FALSE (F). *PRINT THE LETTER OF THE CORRECT ANSWER IN THE SPACE AT THE RIGHT.*

13. To determine the value of the merchandise available for sale, the purchases are added to the beginning merchandise inventory. 13.____

14. The closing merchandise inventory is shown on both the Balance Sheet and the Income and Expense Statement. 14.____

15. The allowance for bad debts account is closed into the income and expense summary account at the close of the fiscal period. 15.____

16. The accounts payable account shows the total amount owed to creditors and also shows how much is owed to each creditor. 16.____

17. Sales discount is usually subtracted from the sales in the Income and Expense Statement. 17.____

18. The use of controlling accounts increases the possibility of errors in preparing the trial balance. 18.____

19. The use of controlling accounts results in fewer accounts in the General Ledger. 19.____

20. The total of the schedule of accounts receivable should equal the balance of the accounts receivable account in the General Ledger. 20.____

21. Closing entries summarize in the income and expense summary account the income costs and expense for the fiscal period. 21.____

22. The post-closing trial balance is made before the Balance Sheet has been made. 22.____

23. The closing entries are recorded in the General Journal. 23.____

24. The debit balance of the equipment account should show the book value of the equipment on hand. 24.____

25. The balance of the allowance for depreciation of equipment account is shown on the Balance Sheet. 25.____

KEY (CORRECT ANSWERS)

1. $3,000
2. $500
3. $8,000
4. $120
5. $300

6. $3,000
7. 3%
8. $22,000
9. April 30
10. Feb. 28

11. $5.00
12. $6.00
13. T
14. T
15. F

16. F
17. T
18. F
19. T
20. T

21. T
22. F
23. T
24. F
25. T

BOOKKEEPING PROBLEMS
EXAMINATION SECTION
TEST 1

DIRECTIONS: Each question or incomplete statement is followed by several suggested answers or completions. Select the one that BEST answers the question or completes the statement. *PRINT THE LETTER OF THE CORRECT ANSWER IN THE SPACE AT THE RIGHT.*

1. The accounts in a general ledger are BEST arranged 1.____

   A. in numerical order
   B. according to the frequency with which each account is used
   C. according to the order in which the headings of the columns in the cash journals are arranged
   D. according to the order in which they are used in preparing financial statements

2. A physical inventory is an inventory obtained by 2.____

   A. an actual count of the items on hand
   B. adding the totals of the stock record cards
   C. deducting the cost of goods sold from the purchases for the period
   D. deducting the purchases from the sales for the period

3. Modern accounting practice favors the valuation of the inventories of a going concern at 3.____

   A. current market prices, if higher than cost
   B. cost or market, whichever is lower
   C. estimated selling price
   D. probable value at forced sale

4. A subsidiary ledger contains accounts which show 4.____

   A. details of contingent liabilities of undetermined amount
   B. totals of all asset accounts in the general ledger
   C. totals of all liability accounts in the general ledger
   D. details of an account in the general ledger

5. A statement of the assets, liabilities, and net worth of a business is called a 5.____

   A. trial balance
   B. budget
   C. profit and loss statement
   D. balance sheet

6. The one of the following which is NEVER properly considered a negotiable instrument is a(n) 6.____

   A. invoice
   B. bond
   C. promissory note
   D. endorsed check

7. The term *current assets* USUALLY includes such things as 7.____

   A. notes payable
   B. machinery and equipment
   C. furniture and fixtures
   D. accounts receivable

8. An accounting system which records revenues as soon as they are earned and records liabilities as soon as they are incurred regardless of the date of payment is said to operate on a(n) ______ basis. 8.____

A. accrual B. budgetary C. encumbrance D. cash

9. A *trial balance* is a list of 9.____

A. the credit balances in all accounts in a general ledger
B. all general ledger accounts and their balances
C. the asset accounts in a general ledger and their balances
D. the liability accounts in a general ledger and their balances

10. A controlling account contains the totals of 10.____

A. the accounts used in preparing the balance sheet at the end of the fiscal period
B. the individual amounts entered in the accounts of a subsidiary ledger during the fiscal period
C. all entries in the general journal during the fiscal period
D. the accounts used in preparing the profit and loss statement for the fiscal period

11. The ESSENTIAL nature of an asset is that it(s) 11.____

A. must be tangible
B. must be easily converted into cash
C. must have value
D. cost must be included in the profit and loss statement

12. When an asset is depreciated on the straight-line basis, the amount charged off for depreciation 12.____

A. is greater in the earlier years of the asset's life
B. is greater in the later years of the asset's life
C. varies each year according to the extent to which the asset is used during the year
D. is equal each full year of the asset's life

Questions 13-27.

DIRECTIONS: Questions 13 to 27 consist of a list of some of the accounts in a general ledger. Indicate whether each account listed generally contains a debit or a credit balance by putting the letter D (for debit balance) or the letter C (for credit balance) in the correspondingly numbered space on the right for each account listed. For example, for the account Cash, which generally contains a debit balance, you would give the letter D as your answer.

13. Sales Taxes Collected 13.____

14. Social Security Taxes Paid by Employer 14.____

15. Deposits from Customers 15.____

16. Freight Inward 16.____

17. Sales Discount 17.____

18. Withholding Taxes Payable 18.____

19. L. Norton, Drawings 19.____

20. Office Salaries 20.____

21. Merchandise Inventory 21.____

22. L. Norton, Capital 22.____

23. Purchases Returns 23.____

24. Unearned Rent Income 24.____

25. Reserve for Bad Debts 25.____

26. Depreciation of Machinery 26.____

27. Insurance Prepaid 27.____

Questions 28-42.

DIRECTIONS: Questions 28 to 42 consist of a list of some of the accounts in a general ledger. For the purpose of preparing financial statements, each of these accounts is to be classified into one of the following five major classifications, lettered A to E, as follows:

A. Assets B. Liabilities C. Proprietorship
D. Income E. Expense

You are to indicate the classification to which each account belongs by printing the correct letter, A, B, C, D, or E, in the correspondingly numbered space on the right. For example, for the account Furniture and Fixtures, which is an asset account, you would print the letter A.

28. Notes Receivable 28.____

29. Sales 29.____

30. Wages Payable 30.____

31. Office Salaries 31.____

32. Capital Stock Authorized 32.____

33. Goodwill 33.____

34. Capital Surplus 34.____

35. Office Supplies Used 35.____

36. Interest Payable 36.____

37. Prepaid Rent 37.____

38. Interest Cost 38.____

39. Accounts Payable 39.____

40. Prepaid Insurance 40.____

41. Merchandise Inventory 41.____

42. Interest Earned 42.____

43. A trial balance will NOT indicate that an error has been made in 43.____

   A. computing the balance of an account
   B. entering an amount in the wrong account
   C. carrying forward the balance of an account
   D. entering an amount on the wrong side of an account

44. Many business firms maintain a book of original entry in which all bills to be paid are recorded. 44.____
This book is known as a

   A. purchase returns journal
   B. subsidiary ledger
   C. voucher register
   D. notes payable register

45. Many business firms provide a petty cash fund from which to pay for small items in order to avoid the issuing of many small checks. 45.____
If this fund is replenished periodically to restore it to its original amount, the fund is called a(n) ______ fund.

   A. imprest
   B. debenture
   C. adjustment
   D. expense reserve

46. A firm which voluntarily terminates business, selling its assets and paying its liabilities, is said to be in 46.____

   A. receivership
   B. liquidation
   C. depletion
   D. amortization

47. The phrase *3%-10 days* on an invoice ORDINARILY means that 47.____

   A. 3% of the amount must be paid each 10 days
   B. the purchaser is entitled to only ten days credit
   C. a discount of 3% will be allowed for payment in 10 days
   D. the entire amount must be paid in 10 days or a penalty of 3% of the amount due will be added

48. The CHIEF disadvantage of *single-entry* bookkeeping is that it 48.____

   A. is too difficult to operate
   B. is illegal for income tax purposes
   C. provides no possibility of determining net profits
   D. furnishes an incomplete picture of the business

49. Sales *minus* cost of goods sold *equals* 49.____

   A. net profit
   B. gross sales
   C. gross profit
   D. net sales

50. The amounts of the transactions recorded in a journal are transferred to the general ledger accounts by a process known as 50.____

A. auditing B. balancing C. posting D. verifying

51. A merchant purchased a stock of goods and priced these goods so as to gain 40% on the cost to him. 51.____
If the merchant sold these goods for $840, the COST of these goods to him was

A. $556 B. $600 C. $348 D. $925

52. In the interest at 6% for one full year on a principal sum amounts to $12, the *principal sum* is 52.____

A. $150 B. $96 C. $196 D. $200

53. On October 17, a business man discounted a customer's 90-day non-interest bearing note at his bank. The face of the note was $960, and it was dated September 28. The discount rate was 5%. 53.____
Using a 360-day year, the amount in cash that the business man received from the bank was MOST NEARLY

A. $899.33 B. $950.67 C. $967.50 D. $989.75

54. A certain correctly totaled cash receipts journal contained the following columns: Net Cash Debit, Accounts Receivable, Sales Discounts, and General. 54.____
At the end of April, the totals of the columns were as follows: Net Cash Debit - $18,925.15, Accounts Receivable (not given), Sales Discounts - $379.65, General - $5,639.25.
The TOTAL of the Accounts Receivable column was

A. $11,194.50 B. $21,344.32 C. $7,621.19 D. $13,665.55

55. In its first year of operation, a retail store had cash sales of $49,000 and installment sales of $41,000. 55.____
If 12% of the amount of these installment sales were collected in that year, the TOTAL amount of cash received from sales was

A. $22,176 B. $34,987 C. $53,920 D. $55,650

56. I. Conklin and J. Ulster formed a partnership and agreed to share profits in proportion to their initial capital investments. I. Conklin invested $15,000 and J. Ulster invested $12,500. 56.____
If the profits for the year were $16,500, J. Ulster's share of the profits was

A. $6,750 B. $7,500 C. $8,100 D. $8,300

57. In a certain city, the tax rate on real estate one year was $48.75 per thousand dollars of assessed valuation. If an apartment house in that city was assessed for $185,000, the real estate tax payable by the owner of that house was MOST NEARLY 57.____

A. $9,018.75 B. $9,009.75 C. $8,900.00 D. $8,905.25

58. A correctly totaled cash payments journal contained the following columns: Net Cash, Accounts Payable, Purchase Discounts, General. At the end of April, the totals of the columns were as follows: Net Cash - $18,375.60, Accounts Payable - $16,981.19, Purchase Discounts (not given), General - $1,875.37. The TOTAL of the Purchase Discounts column was 58.____

A. $120.36 B. $239.87 C. $480.96 D. $670.51

59. On January 1, the credit balance of the Accounts Payable account in a general ledger was $9,139.87. For the month of January, the Purchase Journal total amounted to $3,467.81; the Accounts Payable column in the Cash Disbursements Journal amounted to $2,935.55; the total of the Returned Purchases Journal for January amounted to $173.15; and the Miscellaneous column in the Cash Disbursements Journal showed that $750 had been paid in January on notes given to creditors and entered in previous months. The BALANCE in the Accounts Payable account at the end of January was 59.____

A. $8,437.89 B. $9,498.98 C. $9,998.98 D. $10,132.68

60. The bank statement received from his bank by a business man showed a certain balance for the month of June. This bank statement showed a service charge of $5.19 for the month. He discovered that a check drawn by him in the amount of $83.75 and returned by the bank had been entered on the stub of his checkbook as $38.75. He also found that two checks which he had issued, #29 for $37.18 and #33 for $18.69, were not listed on the statement and had not been returned by the bank. The balance in his checkbook before he reconciled it with the balance shown on the bank statement was $8,917.91. The BALANCE on the bank statement was 60.____

A. $8,903.97 B. $8,923.59 C. $8,997.65 D. $9,303.95

KEY (CORRECT ANSWERS)

1. D	16. D	31. E	46. B
2. A	17. D	32. C	47. C
3. B	18. C	33. A	48. D
4. D	19. D	34. C	49. C
5. D	20. D	35. E	50. C
6. A	21. D	36. B	51. B
7. D	22. C	37. A	52. D
8. A	23. C	38. E	53. B
9. B	24. C	39. B	54. D
10. B	25. C	40. A	55. C
11. C	26. D	41. A	56. B
12. D	27. D	42. D	57. A
13. C	28. A	43. B	58. C
14. D	29. D	44. C	59. B
15. C	30. B	45. A	60. B

TEST 2

Questions 1-25.

DIRECTIONS:
1. Below you will find the general ledger balances on February 28 in the books of C. Dutton.
2. On the following pages, you will find all the entries on the books of C. Dutton for the month of March.
3. In the appropriate spaces on the right, you are to supply the new balances for the accounts called for at the end of March.

The correct balances in the general ledger of C. Dutton on February 28 were as follows: (NOTE: The accounts below have not been arranged in the customary trial balance form.)

Cash	$4,336
Accounts Receivable	8,165
Notes Receivable	2,200
Furniture and Fixtures	9,000
Merchandise Inventory 1/1	4,175
Accounts Payable	5,560
Notes Payable	1,500
Reserve for Depreciation of Furniture and Fixtures	1,800
C. Dutton, Capital	14,162
C. Dutton, Drawing	900
Purchases	42,600
Freight In	36
Rent	1,750
Light	126
Telephone	63
Salaries	4,076
Shipping Expenses	368
Sales	53,200
Sales Biscount	637
Purchase Biscount	596
City Sales Tax Collected	804
Social Security Taxes Payable	96
Withholding Taxes Payable	714

CASH RECEIPTS

Date	Name	Net Cash	Accounts Receivable	Sales Disc.	Miscellaneous Acct.	Miscellaneous Amount
3/1	T. Blint	6,027.00	6,150.00	123.00		
	K . Crowe	1,015.00			Notes Rec.	1,000.00
					Int. Income	15.00
3/10	N. Tandy	3,969.00	4,050.00	81.00		
3/17	Rebuilt Desk Co.	45.00			Furn. & Fixt.	45.00
3/24	J. Walter	2,910.00	3,000.00	90.00		
3/31	National Federal Bank	3,000.00			Notes Payable	3,000.00
		16,966.00	13,200.00	294.00		4,060.00

CASH DISBURSEMENTS

Date		Net Cash	Accts. Pay.	Purch Disc.	Soc. Sec. Tax	With-hold Tax	Miscellaneous Acct.	Amount
3/1	Bliss Realty Co.	875.00					Rent	875.00
3/4	Con. Edison	54.00					Light	54.00
3/10	D. LaRue	2,891.00	2,950.00	59.00				
3/15	Payroll	747.00			26.00	175.	Sal.	948.00
3/19	Rebuilt Desk Co.	115.00					Furn/Fixt	115.00
3/26	Jiggs & Co.	3,686.00	3,800.00	114.00				
3/30	Nat'l Fed Bank	1,218.00					Notes Pay.	1200.00
							Int. Cost	18.00
3/31	Payroll	733.00			22.00	171.	Salary	926.00
3/31	C. Dutton	600.00					Draw	600.00
		10,919.00	6,750.00	173.00	48.00	346.00		4736.00

SALES BOOK

Date	Name	Accts. Rec.	Sales	City Sales Tax
3/3	K. Crowe	6,850.00	6,665.00	185.00
3/10	J. Walters	5,730.00	5,730.00	
3/16	N. Tandy	3,100.00	3,007.00	93.00
3/25	Willis & Co.	7,278.00	7,069.00	209.00
3/30	V. Clyburne	2,190.00	2,190.00	
		25,148.00	24,661.00	487.00

PURCHASE BOOK

Date		Accts. Pay.	Purchases	Freight In	Miscellaneous Acct.	Amount
3/4	Jiggs & Co.	5,212.00	5,070.00	142.00		
3/11	Barton & Co.	320.00			Ins. Prepd.	320.00
3/16	A. Field	6,368.00	6,179.00	189.00		
3/19	Smith Delivery	22.00			Ship. Exp.	22.00
3/23	N.Y. Telephone	29.00			Telephone	29.00
3/26	D. LaRue	3,000.00	3,000.00			
3/29	App & App	7,531.00	7,168.00	363.00		
		22,482.00	21,417.00	694.00		371.00

Supply the balances of the following accounts on March 31 after all posting has been done for March. Put answers in the appropriate spaces on the right. Give amounts only.

1. Cash 1.____
2. Accounts Receivable 2.____
3. Notes Receivable 3.____
4. Insurance Prepaid 4.____
5. Furniture and Fixtures 5.____
6. Accounts Payable 6.____
7. Notes Payable 7.____

8. Reserve for Depreciation of Furniture and Fixtures 8.____
9. C. Dutton, Capital 9.____
10. C. Dutton, Drawing 10.____
11. Purchases 11.____
12. Freight In 12.____
13. Rent 13.____
14. Light 14.____
15. Telephone 15.____
16. Salaries 16.____
17. Shipping Expenses 17.____
18. Sales 18.____
19. Sales Discount 19.____
20. Purchase Discount 20.____
21. City Sales Tax Collected 21.____
22. Social Security Taxes Payable 22.____
23. Withholding Taxes Payable 23.____
24. Interest Income 24.____
25. Interest Cost 25.____

Questions 26-35.

DIRECTIONS: Mr. Adams has a complete set of books - Cash Journals, Purchase and Sales Journals, and a General Journal. Below you will find the General Journal used by Mr. Adams. Under the heading of each money column, you will find a letter of the alphabet. Following the General Journal, there is a series of transactions. You are to determine the correct entry for each transaction and then show on the right in the appropriate space the columns to be used. For example, if a certain transaction results in an entry of $100 in the Notes Receiving Column (on the left side) and an entry of $100 in the General Ledger Column (on the right side), in the appropriate space on the right, you should write A, D. If the record of the transaction requires the use of more than two columns, your answer should contain more than two letters. DO NOT PUT THE AMOUNTS IN YOUR ANSWER SPACE. The LETTERS of the columns to be used are sufficient. If a transaction requires no entry in the General Journal, write *None* in the appropriate space in your answer space, even though a record would be made in some other journal.

GENERAL JOURNAL

Notes Receivable	Accounts Payable	General Ledger	L. F.		General Ledger	Accounts Receivable	Notes Payable
A	B	C			D	E	F

26. We sent Tripp & Co. a 30-day trade acceptance for $500 for merchandise sold him today. They accepted it. 26.____

27. The proprietor, Mr. Adams, returned $100 in cash to be deposited, representing Traveling Expenses he had not used. 27.____

28. An entry in the purchase journal last month for a purchase invoice from V. Valides for $647 was erroneously entered in the purchase journal as $746 and posted as such. 28.____

29. A check for $200 received from Mr. Breen was erroneously credited to account of P. Ungar. 29.____

30. In posting the totals of the cash receipts journal last month, an item of bank discount of $30 on our note for $1500 discounted for 60 days was included in the total posted to the sales discount account. 30.____

31. M. Hogan paid his note of $600 and interest of $12 and his account was credited for $612. 31.____

32. Mr. Blow informed us he could not pay his invoice of $2000 due today. Instead, he sent us his 30-day note for $2000 for 30 days bearing interest at 6% per annum. 32.____

33. The proprietor, Mr. Adams, drew $75 to buy his daughter a U.S. Bond. 33.____

34. Mr. O'Brien wrote to us that we overcharged him on an invoice last week. 34.____

35. Returned $120 worth of merchandise to Pecora & Co. and received their credit memorandum. 35.____

Questions 36-50.

DIRECTIONS: In Questions 36 to 50, you will find a list of accounts with a number before each.

1. Cash
2. Accounts Receivable
3. Notes Receivable
4. Notes Receivable Discounted
5. Furniture and Fixtures
6. Delivery Equipment
7. Insurance Prepaid
8. Depreciation on Delivery Equipment
9. Bad Debts
10. Purchases
11. Discount on Purchases
12. Sales
13. Discount on Sales
14. Accounts Payable
15. Notes Payable
16. Interest Cost
17. Reserve for Depreciation on Delivery Equipment
18. Reserve for Bad Debts
19. Sales Taxes Collected
20. Ben Miller, Capital
21. Ben Miller, Drawing
22. Interest Income
23. Purchase Returns

Using the number in front of each account title (using no accounts not listed), make journal entries for the transactions given below. Do not write the names of the accounts in your answer space. Simply indicate in the proper space on the right the numbers of the accounts to be debited or credited. Always give the number or numbers of the accounts to be debited first, then give the number or numbers of accounts to be credited. For example, if furniture and fixtures and delivery equipment are to be debited, and cash and notes payable are to be credited in a certain transaction, then write in your answer space 5, 6 - 1, 15 (use a dash to separate the debits from the credits).

36. F. Pierce, a customer, went into bankruptcy owing us $600. We received a check for $200. 36.____

37. Later in the month, we are informed that there is no possibility of collecting the balance from F. Pierce. There is a sufficient balance in the Reserve for Bad Debts to take care of the above. 37.____

38. Set up the Depreciation on the Delivery Equipment for the year amounting to $240. 38.____

39. Discounted M. Colby's note for $500 today and received $490 in proceeds. 39.____

40. Mr. Miller, the proprietor, invested $2000 in the business. 40.____

41. Paid our note due to Dillon & Co. today for $800 with interest of $16. 41.____

42. Accepted Finnegan's trade acceptance for $1500 for merchandise bought today. 42.____

43. Create a Reserve for Bad Debts of $2000 at the end of the year. 43.____

44. Returned to Dillon & Co. $30 worth of damaged merchandise for credit. They allowed it. 44.____

45. G. Garry claimed a discount of $12 which we had failed to allow him. He had already paid his bill. Sent him check for $12. 45.____

46. On one sale during the month, we had failed to collect the Sales Tax of $15. Wrote to the customer and he sent us a check for $15. 46.____

47. M. Colby paid his note due today which we had discounted two months ago. 47.____

48. Bought a new safe for $875 from Cramer & Co., terms 2/10, n/60 days. Agreed to pay them in 60 days. 48.____

49. Bought merchandise during the month amounting to $17,500 - all on account. 49.____

50. On December 31, paid for a Fire Insurance policy to run for three years from that date - premium was $480. 50.____

51. The following information was taken from the ledger of Peter Dolan on Dec. 31 after adjusting entries had been posted to the ledger. 51.____

Sales Income	$60,000
Sales Returns	3,500
Mdse. Purchases	42,000
Inventory of 1/1	9,400
Sales Taxes Payable	360
Freight Inward	225
Inventory 12/31	7,640
Insurance Unexpired	163

Find the gross profit on Sales for the year.

52. On March 31, your bank sent you a statement of account. You compared the canceled checks with the stubs in your checkbook and found the following: 52.____

Check #34 - $56.00 had not been paid by the bank
#44 - $38.00 had been paid by the bank as $38.89 because the amount on the check did not agree with your stub in the checkbook
#52 - $76.50 had not been returned by the bank, though the check had been certified
#57 - $127.42 had not been paid by the bank

What total amount would you deduct from the balance on the bank's statement as checks outstanding?

53. On April 30, Mr. Jolley received his statement of account from the bank. A comparison of the bank statement and your checkbook revealed the following: Checkbook balance $5,640; this included a deposit of $325 on the last day of April which had not been entered on the bank statement. 53.____

You also find the following:

Check #69 - $89.00 had not been paid by the bank
#70 - Paid by the bank as $47.55, had been entered in your checkbook as $45.57
#76 - $114.30 had not been paid by the bank

The bank statement included a debit memo of $4.00 for excessive activity during the month.

What was the balance on the bank statement?

54. An invoice dated January 15 for merchandise you bought added up to $876.00. The terms were 3/10, n/60, F.O.B. DESTINATION. When the goods arrived, you paid freight amounting to $8.50. On January 20, you returned goods billed at $26 and received credit therefor. You paid the bill on January 24. 54.____

What was the amount of your check?

55. Income taxes paid by residents of a certain state are based on the balance of taxable income at the following 55.____

rates: 2% on first $1000 or less
3% on 2nd and 3rd $1000
4% on 4th and 5th $1000
5% on 6th and 7th $1000
6% on 8th and 9th $1000
7% on all over $9000

What would be the NORMAL income tax to be paid by a resident of that state whose taxable balance of income was $6,750?

56. A salesman's gross earnings for the year came to $8,820. His rate of Commission was 5% of his sales to customers after deducting returns by customers. During the year, his customers returned 10% of the goods they purchased. What were his total sales during the year before deducting returns? 56.____

57. On December 31, the insurance account contained a debit for $144 for a three-year fire insurance policy dated August 1. What amount should be listed on the balance sheet of December 31 of that year? 57.____

58. A partnership began business on January 1 with partners' investments of $26,000. During the year, the partners drew $18,500 for personal use. On December 31, the assets of the firm were $46,300, and the liabilities were $15,600. What was the firm's net profit for the year? (Write P or L before your answer.) 58.____

59. The rent income account of a real estate firm showed a total balance of $75,640 at the end of 1986. Of this amount, $3,545 represented prepaid 1987 rents. The account also included entries for 1986 rents due from tenants but not yet collected, amounting to $2,400.
What amount should be listed on the profit and loss statement as rent income for 1986? 59.____

60. You discounted a customer's note for $7,200 at your bank at the rate of 6% and received net proceeds of $7,182.
How many days did the note have to run from date of discount to date of maturity? (Use 360 days to the year.) 60.____

Questions 61-90.

DIRECTIONS: In Questions 61 to 90, you will find a list of ledger accounts. Indicate whether an account is generally listed in the Trial Balance as a DEBIT or as a CREDIT by putting the letter *D* or the letter *C* in the correct space on the right for each account listed.

61. Sales 61.____

62. Land 62.____

63. Notes Payable 63.____

64. Traveling Expenses 64.____

65. Purchases 65.____

66. Buildings 66.____

67. Merchandise Inventory 67.____

68. Machinery and Equipment 68.____

69. Notes Receivable 69.____

70. Bonds Payable 70.____

71. Advertising 71.____

72. Delivery Expense 72.____

73. Cash 73.____

74. Accounts Payable 74.____

75. Interest on Bonds 75.____

76. Real Estate Taxes 76.____

77. Accounts Receivable 77.____

78. Don Burch, Proprietor 78.____

79. Sales Discount 79.____

80. Withholding Taxes 80.____

81. Depreciation 81.____

82. Prepaid Insurance 82.____

83. Reserve for Dep. on Buildings 83.____

84. Rent Income 84.____

85. Reserve for Bad Debts 85.____

86. Don Burch, Drawing Account 86.____

87. Sales Returns 87.____

88. Bad Debts 88.____

89. Purchase Discount 89.____

90. Reserve for Dep. on Machinery & Equipment 90.____

KEY (CORRECT ANSWERS)

1.	$ 10,383	31.	C,D,D	61.	C
2.	$ 20,113	32.	A,E	62.	D
3.	$ 1,200	33.	None	63.	C
4.	$ 320	34.	C,E	64.	D
5.	$ 9,070	35.	B,D	65.	D
6.	$ 21,292	36.	1-2	66.	D
7.	$ 3,300	37.	18-2	67.	D
8.	$ 1,800	38.	8-17	68.	D
9.	$ 14,162	39.	1,16-4	69.	D
10.	$ 1,500	40.	1-20	70.	C
11.	$ 64,017	41.	15,16-1	71.	D
12.	$ 730	42.	14-15	72.	D
13.	$ 2,625	43.	9-18	73.	D
14.	$ 180	44.	14-23	74.	C
15.	$ 92	45.	13-1	75.	D
16.	$ 5,950	46.	1-19	76.	D
17.	$ 390	47.	4-3	77.	D
18.	$ 77,861	48.	5-14	78.	C
19.	$ 931	49.	10-14	79.	D
20.	$ 769	50.	7-1	80.	C
21.	$1,291	51.	$12,515	81.	D
22.	$ 144	52.	$ 183.42	82.	D
23.	$1,060	53.	$ 5,512.32	83.	C
24.	$ 15	54.	$ 816	84.	C
25.	$ 18	55.	$ 247.50	85.	C
26.	A-E	56.	$196,000	86.	D
27.	None	57.	$ 124	87.	D
28.	B-D	58.	P $23,200	88.	D
29.	C,E	59.	$72,095	89.	C
30.	C,D	60.	15	90.	C

TEST 3

DIRECTIONS: Each question or incomplete statement is followed by several suggested answers or completions. Select the one that BEST answers the question or completes the statement. *PRINT THE LETTER OF THE CORRECT ANSWER IN THE SPACE AT THE RIGHT.*

1. Of the following taxes, the one which is levied MOST NEARLY in accordance with ability to pay is a(n) ______ tax. 1.____

   A. excise
   B. income
   C. general property
   D. sales

2. When a check has been lost, the bank on which it is drawn should ORDINARILY be notified and instructed to 2.____

   A. stop payment on the check
   B. issue a duplicate of the check
   C. charge the account of the drawer for the amount of the check
   D. certify the check

3. The profit and loss statement prepared for a retail store does NOT ordinarily show 3.____

   A. the cost of goods sold
   B. depreciation of fixtures and equipment
   C. expenditures for salaries of employees
   D. the net worth of the proprietor

4. When two business corporations join their assets and liabilities to form a new corporation, the procedures is called a(n) 4.____

   A. merger
   B. liquidation
   C. receivership
   D. exchange

5. The method of depreciation which deducts an equal amount each full year of an asset's life is called ______ depreciation. 5.____

   A. sum-of-years digits
   B. declining balance
   C. straight-line
   D. service-hours

6. A fixed asset is an asset that 6.____

   A. is held primarily for sale to customers
   B. is used in the conduct of the business until worn out or replaced
   C. is readily convertible into cash
   D. has no definite value

7. The gross profit on sales for a period is determined by 7.____

   A. subtracting the cost of goods sold from the sales
   B. subtracting the sales returns and the discounts on sales from the gross sales
   C. subtracting the sales from the purchases for the period
   D. finding the difference between the inventory of merchandise at the beginning of the period and the inventory of merchandise at the end of the period

8. The term *auditing* refers to the 8.____

   A. entering of amounts from the journals into the general ledger
   B. reconciliation of the accounts in a subsidiary ledger with the controlling account in the general ledger
   C. preparation of a trial balance of the accounts in the general ledger
   D. examination of the general ledger and other records of a concern to determine its true financial condition

9. A voucher register is a 9.____

   A. type of electric cash register
   B. list of customers whose accounts are past due
   C. list of the assets of a business
   D. book in which bills to be paid are recorded

10. The account DISCOUNT ON PURCHASES is *properly* closed directly to the _______ account. 10.____

   A. Accounts Payable
   B. Sales
   C. Purchases
   D. Fixtures

11. The account UNEARNED RENTAL INCOME is *usually* considered a(n) _______ account. 11.____

   A. asset
   B. nominal
   C. capital
   D. liability

12. A controlling account is an account which contains 12.____

   A. the totals of *all* the expense accounts in the general ledger
   B. the total of the amounts entered in the accounts in a subsidiary ledger
   C. the total of the depreciation on fixtures claimed in *all* preceding years
   D. *all* totals of the income and expense accounts before closing to the Profit and Loss account

13. The purpose of the DRAWING account in the general ledger of an individual enterprise is to show the 13.____

   A. salaries paid to the employees
   B. amounts paid to independent contractors for services rendered
   C. amounts taken by the proprietor for his personal use
   D. total of payments made for general expenses of the business

14. The phrase *2%/10 net 30 days* on an invoice ORDINARILY means that 14.____

   A. 2% of the amount must be paid within 30 days
   B. the purchaser must add 2% to the amount of the invoice if he fails to pay within 30 days
   C. the entire amount must be paid within 30 days
   D. the purchaser may deduct 2% from the amount if he pays within 30 days

15. The ESSENTIAL characteristic of a C.O.D. sale of merchandise is that the 15.____

   A. purchaser pays for the merchandise upon its receipt by him
   B. seller guarantees the merchandise to be as specified by him
   C. merchandise is delivered by a common carrier
   D. purchaser is permitted to pay for the merchandise in convenient installments

16. If the drawer of a check makes an error in writing the amount of the check, he should 16.____

A. erase the error and insert the correct amount
B. cross out the error and insert the correct amount
C. destroy the check and prepare another one
D. write the correct amount directly above the incorrect one

17. States do NOT levy a(n) ______ tax. 17.____

A. unemployment insurance
B. income
C. corporation franchise
D. export

18. The cost of goods sold by a retail store is PROPERLY determined by 18.____

A. *adding* the closing inventory to the total of the opening inventory and the purchases for the year
B. *deducting* the closing inventory from the total of the opening inventory and the purchases for the year
C. *deducting* the total of the opening and closing inventories from the purchases for the year
D. *adding* the total of the opening and closing inventories

19. The PRIMARY purpose of a trial balance is to determine 19.____

A. that all transactions have been entered in the journals
B. the accuracy of the totals in the general ledger
C. the correctness of the amounts entered in the journals
D. that amounts have been posted to the proper accounts in the general ledger

20. The SURPLUS account of a corporation is *ordinarily* used to record 20.____

A. the actual amount subscribed by stockholders
B. the amount of profits earned by the corporation
C. any excess of current assets over current liabilities
D. the total of the fixed assets of the corporation

Questions 21-30.

DIRECTIONS: Each of Questions 21 to 30 consists of a typical transaction of Our Business followed by the debit and credit (amounts omitted) of the journal entry for that transaction. For each of these questions, the debit and credit given may be appropriately classified under one of the following categories:

A. The debit of the journal entry is CORRECT but the credit is INCORRECT.
B. The debit of the journal entry is INCORRECT but the credit is CORRECT.
C. BOTH the debit and the credit of the journal entry are correct.
D. BOTH the debit and the credit of the journal entry are incorrect.

Examine each question carefully. Then, in the correspondingly numbered space on the right, mark as your answer the letter preceding the category which is the BEST of the four suggested above.

SAMPLE QUESTION: We purchased a desk for cash.
Debit: Office Equipment
Credit: Accounts Payable

In this example, the debit is correct but the credit is incorrect. Therefore, you should mark A as your answer.

21. We sent a check for $500 to R. Thomas in payment for an invoice for that amount. 21.____
Debit: Cash Credit: Accounts Receivable

22. We took merchandise, amounting to $35, for our own use. 22.____
Debit: Proprietor, Personal Credit: Purchases

23. Arthur Townsend's 90-day note for $350, which was discounted by us at our bank last month, was paid by him today. 23.____
Debit: Notes Receivable Discounted
Credit: Accounts Receivable

24. We sold merchandise to T. Wilson on account of $275. 24.____
Debit: Accounts Payable Credit: Sales

25. We returned damaged merchandise to B. Lowell and received a credit memorandum from him for $28. 25.____
Debit: Accounts Payable
Credit: Sales Returns and Allowances

26. We paid our 30-day note given to Mr. Kane for $650 without interest. 26.____
Debit: Notes Receivable Credit: Cash

27. We sent Chet Carr a check for $10.50 for a discount he had forgotten to take when he paid us for merchandise this week. 27.____
Debit: Sales Discounts Credit: Cash

28. The bank loaned us $1000, and we invested it in the business. 28.____
Debit: Cash Credit: Loan Receivable

29. We recorded depreciation for the year on our office equipment. 29.____
Debit: Reserve for Depreciation of Office Equipment
Credit: Depreciation of Office Equipment

30. One of our customers, Allen Koren, was declared bankrupt and his debt of $25 to us was canceled. 30.____
Debit: Reserve for Bad Debts Credit: Accounts Receivable

Questions 31-45.

DIRECTIONS: Questions 31 to 45 consist of a list of some of the accounts in the general ledger of a corporation which operates a retail store. Indicate whether each account listed contains generally a debit or credit balance by marking the letter D (for debit balance) or the letter C (for credit balance) in the correspondingly numbered space on the right.
For example, for the account Cash, which generally contains a debit balance, you would mark the letter D as your answer.

31. Rent Expense 31.____

32. Allowance for Depreciation of Fixtures 32.____

33. Sales Returns and Allowances 33.____

34. Security Deposit for Electricity 34.____

35. Accrued Salaries Payable 35.____

36. Dividends Payable 36.____

37. Petty Cash Fund 37.____

38. Notes Receivable Discounted 38.____

39. Surplus 39.____

40. Capital Stock Authorized 40.____

41. Insurance Expense 41.____

42. Sales for Cash 42.____

43. Purchase Discounts 43.____

44. Automobile Delivery Equipment 44.____

45. Bad Debts Expense 45.____

Questions 46-60.

DIRECTIONS: Questions 46 to 60 consist of a list of some of the accounts in a general ledger. For the purpose of preparing financial statements, each of these accounts is to be classified into one of the following five major classifications, lettered A to E, as follows:
A. Assets B. Liabilities C. Income D. Expense E. Capital You are to indicate the classification to which each belongs by marking the appropriate letter, A, B, C, D or E. in the correspondingly numbered space on the right. For example, for the account MERCHANDISE INVENTORY, which is an asset account, you would mark the letter A as your answer.

46. Purchases 46.____

47. Prepaid Interest 47.____

48. Cash in Bank 48.____

49. Depreciation of Fixtures 49.____

50. Accounts Receivable 50.____

51. Mortgage Payable 51.____

52. Accrued Interest Receivable 52.____

53. Bad Debts 53.____

54. Insurance Expired 54.____

55. Treasury Stock 55.____

56. Investments 56.____

57. Loan to Partner 57.____

58. Unearned Rent Received 58.____

59. Petty Cash Fund 59.____

60. Loss on Sale of Equipment 60.____

KEY (CORRECT ANSWERS)

1.	B	16.	C	31.	D	46.	D
2.	A	17.	D	32.	C	47.	A
3.	D	18.	B	33.	D	48.	A
4.	A	19.	B	34.	D	49.	D
5.	C	20.	B	35.	C	50.	A
6.	B	21.	D	36.	C	51.	B
7.	A	22.	C	37.	D	52.	A
8.	D	23.	A	38.	C	53.	D
9.	D	24.	B	39.	C	54.	D
10.	C	25.	A	40.	C	55.	E
11.	D	26.	B	41.	D	56.	A
12.	B	27.	C	42.	C	57.	A
13.	C	28.	A	43.	C	58.	B
14.	C	29.	D	44.	D	59.	A
15.	A	30.	C	45.	D	60.	D

EXAMINATION SECTION
TEST 1

DIRECTIONS: Each question or incomplete statement is followed by several suggested answers or completions. Select the one that BEST answers the question or completes the statement. *PRINT THE LETTER OF THE CORRECT ANSWER IN THE SPACE AT THE RIGHT.*

1. A line of a Federal Income Tax Rate Schedule reads: 1.____
over *but not over* *your tax is:*
$6,000 $8,000 $1,130 plus 25% of excess over $6,000.
The income tax due on taxable income of $7,200 is

   A. $1,130 B. $1,430 C. $1,630 D. $1,800

2. We discounted at our bank a customer's promissory note for $3,000. The proceeds were $2,985. 2.____
The CORRECT credit part of the entry to record this transaction is

   A. Notes Payable, $3,000
   B. Notes Receivable Discounted, $3,000
   C. Notes Payable, $2,985
   D. Notes Receivable Discounted, $2,985

3. A payment for gasoline and oil was incorrectly debited to the Delivery Equipment account instead of to the Delivery Expense account. 3.____
This error, if not corrected, would result in

   A. an overstatement of the net profit
   B. an understatement of the net profit
   C. no change in the net profit
   D. no change in the total assets

4. A federal depository receipt is issued when a firm 4.____

   A. reports to an employee the amount of federal taxes withheld from his wages during the year
   B. purchases United States government bonds
   C. deposits its surplus cash in a bank
   D. deposits in a bank FICA taxes and federal withholding taxes

5. As evidence of part ownership in a corporation, a person receives a 5.____

   A. certificate of incorporation
   B. stock certificate
   C. bond
   D. charter

6. One advantage resulting from the use of controlling accounts in the general ledger is that fewer 6.____

   A. bookkeepers are needed to do the work
   B. pages are needed in each journal

C. accounts are needed in the subsidiary ledgers
D. postings are required in the general ledger

7. The proprietor took home an office desk from the business for his personal use. The effect on the fundamental bookkeeping equation is to 7.____

A. *increase* assets, decrease owner's worth
B. *increase* assets, increase liabilities
C. *increase* assets, increase owner's worth
D. *decrease* owner's worth, decrease assets

8. Which can be determined from information found on the Balance Sheet? 8.____

A. Current ratio
B. Ratio of net profit to sales
C. Total operating expenses
D. Total income

9. In recording the amount of State sales tax collected on cash sales, the amount to be credited is 9.____

A. Sales
B. Sales Taxes Payable
C. Sales Taxes Receivable
D. Sales Taxes Expense

10. The rate of return on capital investment is found by dividing the amount of investment into 10.____

A. total sales
B. proprietor's drawings
C. net income
D. total current assets

Questions 11-15.

DIRECTIONS: Questions 11 through 15 are to be answered on the basis of the following account.

Name *Grey-Jackson, Inc.* Terms: *2/10, N/30*
Address *75 E. 43, New York, N.Y. 10017*

DATE		EXPLANATION	POST. REF.	DEBIT	CREDIT	BALANCE
May	3		S 21	630.00		630.00
	7		Mg 11		25.00	605.00
	10		CR34		605.00	
June	13		S 32	230.00		230.00
	15		Yg 27	15.00		245.00

11. This account will be found in 11.____

A. Accounts Receivable Subsidiary
B. Accounts Payable Subsidiary
C. General
D. Sales

12. From which business paper did the entry on May 3 originate? A 12.____

A. purchases invoice
B. shipping memo
C. sales invoice
D. statement of account

13. The MOST probable reason for the entry on May 7 is that 13.____

A. a partial payment was made
B. merchandise was returned
C. a cash discount on the transaction of May 3 was allowed
D. shipping charges were prepaid

14. In order to obtain more information regarding the entry of May 7, the bookkeeper should refer to 14.____

A. invoice number 11
B. page 11 of the Grey-Jackson, Inc. file
C. the 11th entry in the General Journal
D. page 11 of the General Journal

15. If the debit on June 15 represents a freight charge, how much should be paid on June 22? 15.____

A. $245.00
B. $240.40
C. $240.10
D. $230.00

16. Which error will cause the Trial Balance to be out of balance? The 16.____

A. bookkeeper charged an item to Miscellaneous Expense instead of to Advertising Expense
B. bookkeeper failed to post an entire entry from the General Journal
C. bookkeeper incorrectly entered the amount of a purchase into the Purchases Journal
D. Petty Cash account was omitted from the Trial Balance

17. On October 14, the bookkeeper received in the mail a customer's check for $500. The identical amount, $500, is also due to a creditor on October 14. Which is the recommended bookkeeping procedure? 17.____

A. Endorse the check to the creditor, and mail it to him.
B. Request your firm's bank to certify the customer's cheek, and mail it to your creditor.
C. Deposit the customer's check, and mail a separate check to the creditor.
D. Return the customer's check to him, and request him to mail it to the creditor.

18. A sale is made on June 16, terms 2/10, EOM. In order for the discount to be allowed, payment must be made no later than 18.____

A. June 26
B. June 30
C. July 2
D. July 10

19. When a petty cash fund is established, the effect on the fundamental accounting equation is that total assets 19.____

A. and total liabilities remain unchanged
B. decrease; total liabilities increase

C. decrease; proprietorship decreases
D. increase; proprietorship increases

20. One of the reasons for preparing a Schedule of Accounts Receivable is to 20.____

A. make up statements of customers accounts
B. determine if the subsidiary ledger agrees with the controlling account
C. determine the worth of the business
D. determine the total sales for the fiscal period

21. The current price of a share of stock traded on the stock exchange is called the _______ value. 21.____

A. market B. par C. book D. face

22. In a certain industry, firm A had a current ratio of 4:1; while firm B had a current ratio of 1:1. 22.____
A logical conclusion would be that firm A

A. had a higher merchandise turnover than firm B
B. had more cash than firm B
C. had more assets than firm B
D. was better able to pay its current debts than firm B

23. When a bank certifies a $100 check for the person who wrote the check, it 23.____

A. pays $100 to the person who wrote the check
B. tells the depositor that he should remember this check so as to avoid overdrawing his account
C. immediately deducts the $100 from the balance of the account
D. asks the depositor for $100 to cover the check

24. A 90-day, 6% interest-bearing note for $340 was paid on the due date. 24.____
The amount of the check was

A. $345.10 B. $343.40 C. $340.00 D. $334.90

25. The declaration by a corporation of dividend to be paid at a future date results in a decrease in 25.____

A. assets and a decrease in net worth
B. assets and an increase in liabilities
C. liabilities and a decrease in net worth
D. net worth and an increase in liabilities

KEY (CORRECT ANSWERS)

1.	B	11.	A
2.	B	12.	D
3.	A	13.	B
4.	D	14.	D
5.	B	15.	B
6.	D	16.	D
7.	D	17.	B
8.	A	18.	D
9.	B	19.	A
10.	C	20.	B

21. A
22. D
23. C
24. A
25. D

TEST 2

DIRECTIONS: Each question or incomplete statement is followed by several suggested answers or completions. Select the one that BEST answers the question or completes the statement. *PRINT THE LETTER OF THE CORRECT ANSWER IN THE SPACE AT THE RIGHT.*

1. Which can be determined from information found on the Balance Sheet? 1.____

   A. Current ratio
   B. Rate of net profit based on sales
   C. Merchandise turnover
   D. Total operating expenses

2. Which statement BEST describes the function of a source document in an automatic data processing system? 2.____

   A. Input is recorded on it.
   B. Output is recorded on it.
   C. Raw data is obtained from it.
   D. It manipulates the central processing unit.

3. Postings to the debit side of Accounts Payable in the General Ledger USUALLY come from the ______ Journal. 3.____

   A. Cash Payments B. Sales
   C. Purchases D. Cash Receipts

4. The PRIMARY purpose of a trial balance is to 4.____

   A. check the accuracy of control accounts
   B. locate errors in posting
   C. assure the accuracy of financial reports
   D. determine if the general ledger is in balance

5. An outstanding check is a check that has 5.____

   A. been voided B. been deposited
   C. not been written D. not been paid

6. If the total of the credit column on the Income Statement of the worksheet is larger than the total of the debit column, the difference is called net 6.____

   A. income B. loss C. worth D. value

7. Which is NOT an input device in an electronic data processing system? A(n) 7.____

   A. optical scanner B. magnetic tape unit
   C. printer D. console keyboard

8. After all closing entries are recorded and posted, the ______ account would still have a balance. 8.____

   A. Income and Expense Summary B. Purchases
   C. Owner's Drawing D. Owner's Capital

9. Failure to replenish Petty Cash at the end of the fiscal period will result in 9.____

A. *understatement* of Net Income
B. *overstatement* of Net Income
C. *understatement* of Petty Cash
D. *overstatement* of Expenses

10. Which item should NOT appear on a job application form? 10.____

A. Current address
B. Social security number
C. Religion
D. Education

11. If a person holds a civil service job, he or she is employed by 11.____

A. the government
B. a private accounting firm
C. a large engineering firm
D. a nonprofit charitable organization

12. Which is NOT given by an employer to an employee as a fringe benefit? 12.____

A. Paid vacation days
B. Paid sick leave
C. Group life insurance coverage
D. Payment of federal income taxes

13. A source of current job openings is(are) 13.____

A. DICTIONARY OF OCCUPATIONAL TITLES
B. CAREER INFORMATION HANDBOOK
C. classified advertisements in a newspaper
D. OCCUPATIONAL OUTLOOK HANDBOOK

14. Which reason should NOT generally be used by an employer when making a hiring decision? 14.____
An applicant('s)

A. resume reveals a lack of job-related skills
B. attendance record on a previous job is poor
C. has improperly prepared the job application
D. is married

15. When listing previous jobs on an employment application, the prospective employer should list his/her _______ job first. 15.____

A. least recent
B. most recent
C. favorite
D. highest salaried

16. The LEAST appropriate reference on an application for a job would be a 16.____

A. relative
B. guidance counselor
C. former employer
D. prominent member of the community

17. Receipt of a $300 check from a customer in payment of his $300 account results in 17.____

    A. an increase in total value of assets
    B. a decrease in total value of assets
    C. no change in total value of assets
    D. an increase in net worth

18. The monthly report sent to each customer to remind him of the amount he owes is called a(n) 18.____

    A. invoice
    B. statement of account
    C. bank statement
    D. credit memorandum

19. Entries in the Cash Payments Journal are USUALLY made from 19.____

    A. Sales Invoices
    B. Petty Cash Vouchers
    C. Checkbook stubs
    D. Purchase orders

20. The Petty Cash book shows a petty cash balance of $10 on June 30. An actual count of the petty cash on hand on June 30 shows $9.00 in the petty cash box. 20.____
The account to be debited to record the difference between the book balance and the petty cash on hand would be

    A. Petty Cash
    B. Cash
    C. Cash Short and Over
    D. Petty Cash Expense

KEY (CORRECT ANSWERS)

1.	A	11.	A
2.	C	12.	D
3.	A	13.	C
4.	D	14.	D
5.	D	15.	B
6.	A	16.	A
7.	C	17.	C
8.	D	18.	B
9.	B	19.	C
10.	C	20.	C

TEST 3

DIRECTIONS: Each question or incomplete statement is followed by several suggested answers or completions. Select the one that BEST answers the question or completes the statement. *PRINT THE LETTER OF THE CORRECT ANSWER IN THE SPACE AT THE RIGHT.*

1. Information prepared in machine-readable form for processing by automatic data processing equipment is commonly referred to as 1.____

   A. output B. business data
   C. input D. financial data

2. Mr. H. Brown, the owner of a small business, withdrew money for his own use. The bookkeeper debited the H. Brown Capital account and credited the Cash account. To correct this error, the bookkeeper should debit the ______ account and credit the ______ account. 2.____

   A. H. Brown Personal; H. Brown Capital
   B. H. Brown Personal; Cash
   C. Cash; H. Brown Personal
   D. H. Brown Capital; H. Brown Personal

3. The Dale Corporation earned a net profit of $50,000 for the year. Before closing the books, the Capital Stock account showed a balance of $300,000, and the Retained Earnings account had a balance of $40,000.
   The net worth of the firm on December 31 was 3.____

   A. $340,000 B. $350,000 C. $390,000 D. $310,000

4. Of the following examples of computer programs, the one most commonly associated with standard bookkeeping procedures is 4.____

   A. Microsoft Word B. Adobe Acrobat Pro
   C. Microsoft PowerPoint D. Microsoft Excel

5. The receipt of a check in settlement of an interest-bearing note will result in an increase in assets(,) 5.____

   A. and a decrease in assets
   B. a decrease in assets, and an increase in capital
   C. a decrease in assets, and a decrease in capital
   D. a decrease in liabilities, and an increase in capital

6. A sale on credit to George Rogers for $200 was incorrectly posted to his account as $20. This error would mean that the 6.____

   A. Schedule of Accounts Receivable would be understated
   B. Accounts Receivable controlling account would be overstated
   C. Schedule of Accounts Receivable would be overstated
   D. trial balance would not balance

7. A cash sale of $250 worth of merchandise subject to a 6% sales tax should be recorded as a debit to the Cash account for 7.____

A. $250 and a credit to the Sales Income account for $250
B. $265 and a credit to the Sales Income account for $265
C. $250, a debit to the Sales Tax Expense account for $15, and a credit to the Sales Income account for $265
D. a credit to the Sales Income account for $250, and a credit to the Sales Taxes Payable account for $15

8. To determine which checks are outstanding at the end of each month, the bookkeeper should 8.____

A. ask the bank to send a list of these outstanding checks
B. find the necessary information in the bank statement
C. compare the cancelled checks with the bank statement
D. compare the cancelled checks with the checkbook stubs

9. An error was made in writing the amount of a check. The BEST business procedure to be followed is to 9.____

A. cross off the incorrect amount on the check and neatly write the correct amount above the incorrect figure
B. erase the incorrect amount on the check and neatly fill in the correct amount
C. write *void* across the check and the stub and write a new check
D. tear up the check and write a new check

10. When a posting machine is used, Accounts Receivable and Accounts Payable are USUALLY kept in a 10.____

A. bound ledger with money columns for debit and credit
B. looseleaf ledger with money columns for debit and credit
C. card ledger with money columns for debit, credit, and balance
D. bound ledger with money columns for debit, credit, and balance

11. The federal individual income tax return MUST be filed by 11.____

A. December 31 B. March 15
C. April 15 D. June 30

12. When cash is received as a result of sales, the PROPER business procedure is to 12.____

A. put the cash in the petty cash box
B. deposit the cash in a checking account at the end of the day
C. deposit the cash in a savings account at the end of the day
D. use the cash to pay current bills

13. Which of the following is computer software used for bookkeeping purposes? 13.____

A. Adobe InDesign B. Microsoft Outlook
C. Adobe Dreamweaver D. Sage 50

14. The bookkeeper failed to record depreciation for the year. As a result, the 14.____

A. assets will be understated
B. profit will be understated
C. profit will be overstated
D. liabilities will be overstated

15. The TOTAL of the Schedule of Accounts Receivable should agree with the 15.____

A. total of the Accounts Receivable column in the cash receipts journal
B. total of the Accounts Receivable column in the general journal
C. balance of the Accounts Receivable controlling account
D. balance in the Sales account

16. Which error would cause the trial balance to be out of balance? 16.____

A. Incorrectly totaling the Sales Journal
B. Failing to post to a customer's account from the Sales Journal
C. Incorrectly debiting the Office Expense account instead of the Furniture and Fixtures account
D. Incorrectly adding the debits in the Notes Payable account

17. The business paper which is used as a source for an entry in the Petty Cash book is a 17.____

A. voucher
B. purchase order
C. check stub
D. credit memorandum

18. On December 31, the Capital Stock account of the Rogers Corporation showed a balance of $75,000, and the Retained Earnings account showed a balance of $15,000. If 1,000 shares of stock were in the hands of stockholders, the book value of each share of stock was 18.____

A. $90 B. $75 C. $60 D. 15

19. A 60-day promissory note dated July 7 will be due on 19.____

A. August 6
B. September 5
C. September 6
D. September 7

20. A bank reconciliation showed a deposit in transit, a bank charge, outstanding checks, and a certified outstanding check. 20.____
On the basis of this information, the bookkeeper should make an entry to record the

A. deposit in transit
B. bank charge
C. outstanding checks
D. certified outstanding check

21. Merchandise was sold on February 8 for $175 less a trade discount of 20%, terms 2/10, n/30. 21.____
The amount of the check received on March 9 should be

A. $137.20 B. $140.00 C. $171.50 D. $175.00

22. The monthly report sent by a bank to a depositor showing his balance in the bank, deposits made during the month, and checks paid during the month is called a 22.____

A. bank reconciliation
B. monthly report
C. bank statement
D. balance sheet

23. A $200 check received from John Howard, a customer, in payment of his $200 promissory note was entered incorrectly by debiting the Cash account and crediting the John Howard account. 23.____
The CORRECTING entry should debit the ______ account and credit the ______ account.

A. Cash; Notes Receivable
B. Notes Receivable; John Howard
C. John Howard; Notes Receivable
D. Cash; John Howard

24. Bond holders of a corporation are ______ of the corporation. 24.____

A. owners B. creditors C. customers D. directors

25. Which error will cause the trial balance to be out of balance? 25.____

A. Posting to the wrong side of a customer's account in the Accounts Receivable Ledger
B. Failure to record a sale in the Sales Journal
C. Totaling the Purchase Journal incorrectly
D. Posting a $1,450 debit to the Accounts Payable controlling account as $1,540

KEY (CORRECT ANSWERS)

1.	C	11.	C
2.	A	12.	B
3.	C	13.	D
4.	D	14.	C
5.	B	15.	C
6.	A	16.	D
7.	D	17.	A
8.	D	18.	A
9.	C	19.	B
10.	C	20.	B

21. B
22. C
23. C
24. B
25. D

EXAMINATION SECTION
TEST 1

DIRECTIONS: Each question or incomplete statement is followed by several suggested answers or completions. Select the one that BEST answers the question or completes the statement. *PRINT THE LETTER OF THE CORRECT ANSWER IN THE SPACE AT THE RIGHT.*

1. You have recently been assigned to a new office and are expected to supervise six clerks. 1.____
All of the following would be good introductory steps to take EXCEPT

   A. giving a clear presentation of yourself to the clerks, including a short summary of your recent work experience
   B. initiating informal discussions with each clerk concerning his work
   C. making a general survey of all the functions which each clerk has been performing
   D. making a list of the duties each clerk is required to perform and giving it to the clerk

2. Your supervisor has advised you that a specific aspect of a job is being done incorrectly and you acknowledge the mistake. 2.____
Of the following, the MOST efficient way of dealing with this situation is to

   A. call a meeting of the clerks who are performing this particular function and explain the correct method
   B. assume the blame and correct the errors as they are given to you
   C. speak with each clerk individually and carefully show each one the proper method
   D. distribute a set of written instructions covering all clerical procedures to the employees doing that particular job

3. A new department regulation calls for a change in a particular method of processing new applications. Two clerks have complained to you that the new method is more time-consuming, and they prefer to do it the original way. 3.____
Of the following, what is the MOST advisable thing to do?

   A. Discuss the situation with them and attempt to determine whether they are utilizing the method properly.
   B. Discuss the advantages of both methods with them and let them use the one that is more practical.
   C. Firmly instruct the clerks to proceed with the new method since it is not up to them to refute department policy.
   D. Tell them to survey the opinions of the other clerks on this matter and inform you of the results.

4. A member of the clerical staff has recently begun reporting late for work rather regularly. On each occasion, the individual presented an excuse, but the latenesses continue. 4.____
Of the following, the MOST advisable action for her supervisor to take is to

   A. have a staff meeting and stress the importance of being on time for work, without singling out the specific individual
   B. put a notice on the departmental office bulletin board, specifying and stressing that lateness can not be tolerated

C. talk privately with the individual to determine whether there are any unusual circumstances that might be causing the lateness
D. send the individual a memorandum clearly indicating that continual lateness will result in disciplinary action

5. Assume that, as the supervisor of a unit, you have been asked to prepare a vacation schedule for your subordinate employees. The employees have had different lengths of service. Some of them have already submitted requests for certain weeks. Of the following, which factor would be LEAST important in setting up this schedule? 5.____

A. Your opinion of each employee's past work performance
B. Each employee's preference for a vacation period
C. The amount of work the unit is expected to accomplish during the vacation period
D. The number of employees who have requested to go on vacation at the same time

6. Your superior finds that he must leave the office one day before he has had time to check and sign the day's correspondence. He asks you to proofread the letters, have corrections made where necessary, and then sign his name. You have never signed his name before. Of the following, the BEST thing for you to do is to 6.____

A. sign your superior's name in full, making it look as much like his handwriting as possible
B. sign your superior's name and your own name in full as proof that you signed for him
C. sign your superior's name in full and add your initials to show that the signature is not his own
D. politely refuse to sign his name because it is forgery

7. The head of your office sometimes makes handwritten notations on original letters which he receives and requests that you mail the letters back to the sender. Of the following, the BEST action for you to take FIRST is to 7.____

A. request that this practice be stopped because it does not provide for a record in the files
B. request that this practice be stopped because it is not the customary way to respond to letters
C. photocopy the letters so that there are copies for the file and then send the letters out
D. ask the head of your office if he wants you to keep any record of the letters

8. The main function of most agency administrative offices is *information management.* Information that is received by an administrative office may be classified as active (information which requires the recipient to take some action) or passive (information which does not require action). Which one of the following items received must clearly be treated as ACTIVE information? A(n) 8.____

A. confirmation of payment
B. press release concerning an agency event
C. advertisement for a new restaurant opening near the agency
D. request for a student transcript

9. Which of the following statements about the use of the photocopy process is CORRECT? 9.____

   A. It is difficult to use.
   B. It can be used to reproduce color.
   C. It does not print well on colored paper.
   D. Once source documents have been used, they cannot be used again.

10. In order to get the BEST estimate of how long a repetitive office procedure should take, a supervisor should find out how 10.____

   A. long it takes her best worker to do the procedure once on a typical day
   B. long it takes her best and worst workers to do the procedure once on a typical day
   C. much time her best worker spends on the procedure during a typical week and the total number of times the worker executes the procedure during the same week
   D. much time all her subordinates spend on the procedure during a typical week and the total number of times the procedure was executed during the same week by all employees

11. Of the following, the MOST suitable and appropriate way to make 250 copies of a particular form is to 11.____

   A. print all 250 copies on the office computer
   B. delegate the work to someone else
   C. reproduce it on a photocopying machine
   D. use an offset printing process

Questions 12-18.

DIRECTIONS: Questions 12 through 18 are to be answered on the basis of the extracts shown below from Federal withholding tables. These tables indicate the amounts which must be withheld from the employee's salary by his employer for Federal income tax and for social security. They are based on weekly earnings.

INCOME TAX WITHHOLDING TABLE

The wages are -		And the number of withholding exemptions claimed is-					
At least	But less than	0	1	2	3	4	5
		The amount of income tax to be withheld shall be -					
$200	$205	$14.10	$11.80	$ 9.50	$ 7.20	$ 4.90	$2.80
205	210	14.90	12.60	10.30	8.00	5.70	3.50
210	215	15.70	13.40	11.10	8.80	6.50	4.20
215	220	16.50	14.20	11.90	9.60	7.30	5.00
220	225	17.30	15.00	12.70	10.40	8.10	5.80
225	230	18.10	15.80	13.50	11.20	8.90	6.60
230	235	18.90	16.60	14.30	12.00	9.70	7.40
235	240	19.70	17.40	15.10	12.80	10.50	8.20
240	245	20.50	18.20	15.90	13.60	11.30	9.00
245	250	21.30	19.00	16.70	14.40	12.10	9.80

SOCIAL SECURITY EMPLOYEE TAX TABLE

Wages		Tax to be withheld	Wages		Tax to be withheld
At least	But less than		At least	But less than	
$202.79	$202.99	$15.35	$229.72	$229.91	$16.75
202.99	203.18	15.36	229.91	230.10	16.76
203.18	203.37	15.37	230.10	230.29	16.77
203.37	203.56	15.38	230.29	230.49	16.78
203.56	203.75	15.39	230.49	230.68	16.79
203.75	203.95	15.40	230.68	230.87	16.80
203.95	204.14	15.41	230.87	231.06	16.81
204.14	204.33	15.42	231.06	231.25	16.82
204.33	204.52	15.43	231.25	231.45	16.83
204.52	204.72	15.44	231.45	231.64	16.84

Wages		Tax to be withheld	Wages		Tax to be withheld
At least	But less than		At least	But less than	
$222.02	$222.22	$16.35	$234.52	$234.72	$17.00
222.22	222.41	16.36	234.72	234.91	17.01
222.41	222.60	16.37	234.91	235.10	17.02
222.60	222.79	16.38	235.10	235.29	17.03
222.79	222.99	16.39	235.29	235.49	17.04
222.99	223.18	16.40	235.49	235.68	17.05
223.18	223.37	16.41	235.68	235.87	17.06
223.37	223.56	16.42	235.87	236.06	17.07
223.56	223.75	16.43	236.06	236.25	17.08
223.75	223.95	16.44	236.25	236.45	17.09

12. Dave Andes has wages of $242.75 for one week. He has claimed three withholding exemptions. 12.____
What is the Federal income tax which should be withheld?

A. $13.60 B. $15.90 C. $18.20 D. $20.50

13. Mary Hodes has wages of $229.95 for one week. 13.____
What is the Social Security tax which should be withheld?

A. $16.75 B. $16.76 C. $16.77 D. $16.78

14. Joe Jones had wages of $235.63 for one week. He has claimed two withholding exemptions. 14.____
What is the Federal income tax which should be withheld?

A. $12.80 B. $14.30 C. $15.10 D. $17.40

15. Tom Stein had wages of $203.95 for one week. What is the Social Security tax which should be withheld? 15.____

A. $15.40 B. $15.41 C. $16.05 D. $16.06

16. Robert Helman had wages of $222.80 for one week. He has claimed one withholding exemption. 16.____
If only Federal income tax and Social Security tax were deducted from his earnings for the same week, how much *take-home* pay should he have for the week?

A. $191.41 B. $193.96 C. $194.12 D. $195.65

17. Audrey Stein has wages of $203.00 for one week. She claimed no withholding exemptions. 17.____
If only Federal income tax and Social Security tax were deducted from her earnings for the same week, how much *take-home* pay should she have for the week?

A. $171.84 B. $172.34 C. $173.54 D. $175.84

18. Anthony Covallo, who worked 28 hours in the past week, has a regular hourly rate of $7.25 per hour and earns a premium of time and a half for hours over 40. He has claimed four withholding exemptions. 18.____
After Social Security tax and Federal income tax are deducted from his wages for the past week, how much pay does he have left?

A. $180.98 B. $181.13 C. $182.29 D. $182.74

19. In judging the adequacy of a standard office form, which of the following is LEAST important? 19.____
_______ of the form.

A. Date B. Legibility C. Size D. Design

20. Clear and accurate telephone messages should be taken for employees who are out of the office. 20.____
Which of the following is of LEAST importance when taking a telephone message?

A. Name of the person called
B. Name of the caller

C. Details of the message
D. Time of the call

21. Suppose that all office supplies are kept in a centrally located cabinet in the office. Of the following, which is usually the BEST policy to adhere to for distribution of supplies? 21.____

A. Permit employees to stock up on all supplies to avoid frequent trips to the cabinet.
B. Assign one employee to be in charge of distributing all supplies to other employees at frequent intervals.
C. Inform employees that supplies should be taken in large quantities and only when needed.
D. Keep cabinet closed and instruct employees that they must check with you before taking supplies.

Questions 22-25.

DIRECTIONS: Questions 22 through 25 are to be answered SOLELY on the basis of the following passage.

Use of the systems and procedures approach to office management is revolutionizing the supervision of office work. This approach views an enterprise as an entity which seeks to fulfill definite objectives. Systems and procedures help to organize repetitive work into a routine, thus reducing the amount of decision-making required for its accomplishment. As a result, employees are guided in their efforts and perform only necessary work. Supervisors are relieved of any details of execution and are free to attend to more important work. Establishing work guides which require that identical tasks be performed the same way each, time permits standardization of forms, machine operations, work methods, and controls. This approach also reduces the probability of errors. Any error committed is usually discovered quickly because the incorrect work does not meet the requirement of the work guides. Errors are also reduced through work specialization which allows each employee to become thoroughly proficient in a particular type of work. Such proficiency also tends to improve the morale of the employees.

22. Of the following, which one BEST expresses the main theme of the above passage? The 22.____

A. advantages and disadvantages of the systems and procedures approach to office management
B. effectiveness of the systems and procedures approach to office management in developing skills
C. systems and procedures approach to office management as it relates to office costs
D. advantages of the systems and procedures approach to office management for supervisors and office workers

23. Work guides are LEAST likely to be used when 23.____

A. standardized forms are used
B. a particular office task is distinct and different from all others
C. identical tasks are to be performed in identical ways
D. similar work methods are expected from each employee

24. According to the above passage, when an employee makes a work error, it USUALLY 24.____

A. is quickly corrected by the supervisor
B. necessitates a change in the work guides
C. can be detected quickly if work guides are in use
D. increases the probability of further errors by that employee

25. The above passage states that the accuracy of an employee's work is INCREASED by 25.____

A. using the work specialization approach
B. employing a probability sample
C. requiring him to shift at one time into different types of tasks
D. having his supervisor check each detail of work execution

KEY (CORRECT ANSWERS)

1.	D	11.	C
2.	A	12.	A
3.	A	13.	B
4.	C	14.	C
5.	A	15.	B
6.	C	16.	A
7.	D	17.	C
8.	D	18.	D
9.	B	19.	A
10.	D	20.	D

21. B
22. D
23. B
24. C
25. A

TEST 2

DIRECTIONS: Each question or incomplete statement is followed by several suggested answers or completions. Select the one that BEST answers the question or completes the statement. *PRINT THE LETTER OF THE CORRECT ANSWER IN THE SPACE AT THE RIGHT.*

1. A certain supervisor often holds group meetings with subordinates to discuss the goals of the unit and manpower requirements for meeting objectives. 1.____
For the supervisor to hold such meetings is a

   A. *good* practice because it will aid both the supervisor and subordinates in planning and completing the unit's work
   B. *good* practice because it will prevent future problems from interfering with the unit's objectives
   C. *poor* practice because the supervisor has the sole responsibility for meeting objectives and should make manpower decisions without any advice
   D. *poor* practice because the subordinates will be allowed to set their own work quotas

2. Assume that you are a supervisor who has been asked to evaluate the work of a clerk who was transferred to your unit about six months ago. 2.____
Which one of the following, by itself, provides the BEST basis for making such an evaluation?

   A. Ask the clerk's former supervisor about the employee's previous work.
   B. Ask the clerk's co-workers for their opinions of the employee's work.
   C. Evaluate the quantity and quality of the employee's work over the six-month period.
   D. Observe the employee's performance from time to time during the next week and base your evaluation on these observations.

3. Which of the following would be the MOST desirable way for a supervisor to help improve the job performance of a particular subordinate? 3.____

   A. Criticize the employee's performance in front of other employees.
   B. Privately warn the employee that failure to meet work standards may lead to dismissal.
   C. Hold a meeting with this employee and other subordinates in which the need to improve the unit's performance is stressed.
   D. Meet privately with the employee and discuss both positive and negative aspects of the employee's work

4. Suppose that your office has a limited supply of a pamphlet which people may read in your office when they seek certain information, but another office in your building is supposed to have a large supply available for distribution to the public. 4.____
Which of the following would be the BEST thing for you to do when someone states that he has not been able to obtain one of these pamphlets?

   A. Tell him that he misunderstood the directions that other employees have given him and carefully direct him to the other office.
   B. Ask whether he has visited the other office and requested a copy from them.
   C. Let him take one of your office's copies of the pamphlet and then call the other office and ask why they have run out of copies for distribution.

D. Tell him that your office does its best to keep the public informed but that this might not be true of other offices.

5. On Monday, a clerk made many errors in completing a new daily record form. The supervisor explained the errors and had the clerk correct the form. On Tuesday, the clerk made fewer errors. Because he was very busy, the supervisor did not point out the errors to the clerk but corrected the errors himself. On Wednesday, the clerk made the same number of errors as on Tuesday. The supervisor reprimanded the clerk for making so many errors. 5.____
The supervisor's handling of this situation on Wednesday may be considered poor MAINLY because the

A. clerk was not given enough time to complete each form properly
B. supervisor should not have expected improvement without further training
C. clerk was obviously incapable of completing the form
D. supervisor should have continued to correct the errors himself

Questions 6-8.

DIRECTIONS: Questions 6 through 8 are to be answered SOLELY on the basis of the information contained in the following passage.

When using words like company, association, *council, committee, and board in place of the full official name, the writer should not capitalize these short forms unless he intends them to invoke the full force of the institution's authority. In legal contracts, in minutes, or in formal correspondence where one is speaking formally and officially on behalf of the company, the term "Company" is usually capitalized, but in ordinary usage, where it is not essential to load the short form with this significance, capitalization would be excessive. (Example: The company will have many good openings for graduates this June.)*

The treatment recommended for short forms of place names is essentially the same as that recommended for short forms of organizational names. In general, we capitalize the full form but not the short form. If Park Avenue is referred to in one sentence, then "the avenue" is sufficient in subsequent references. The same is true with words like building, hotel, station, and airport, which are capitalized when part of a proper name (Pan Am Building, Hotel Plaza, Union Station, O'Hare Airport) but are simply lower-cased when replacing these specific names.

6. The above passage states that USUALLY the short forms of names of organizations 6.____

A. and places should not be capitalized
B. and places should be capitalized
C. should not be capitalized, but the short forms of names of places should be capitalized
D. should be capitalized, but the short forms of names of places should not be capitalized

7. The above passage states that in legal contracts, in minutes, and in formal correspondence, the short forms of names of organizations should 7.____

A. usually not be capitalized
B. usually be capitalized
C. usually not be used
D. never be used

8. It can be INFERRED from the above passage that decisions regarding when to capitalize certain words 8.____

A. should be left to the discretion of the writer
B. should be based on generally accepted rules
C. depend on the total number of words capitalized
D. are of minor importance

9. The Central Terminal and the Gardens Terminal are located on Glover Street. 9.____
In ordinary usage, if this sentence were to be followed by the sentence in the choices below, which form of the sentence would be CORRECT?

A. Both Terminals are situated on the same street.
B. Both terminals are situated on the same Street.
C. Both terminals are situated on the same street.
D. Both Terminals are situated on the same Street.

10. A stylus is a(n) 10.____

A. implement for writing containing a cylinder of graphite
B. implement for writing with ink or a similar fluid
C. pointed implement used to write
D. stick of colored wax used for writing

11. As a supervisor, you have the responsibility of teaching new employees the functions and procedures of your office after their orientation by the personnel office. 11.____
Of the following, the BEST way to begin such instruction is to

A. advise the new employee of the benefits and services available to him, over and above his salary
B. discuss the negative aspects of the departmental procedures and indicate methods available to overcome them
C. assist the new employee in understanding the general purpose of the office procedures and how they fit in with the overall operation
D. give a detailed briefing of the operations of your office, its functions and procedures

12. Assume that you are the supervisor of a clerical unit. One of the duties of the employees in your unit is to conduct a brief interview with persons using the services of your agency for the first time. The purpose of the interview is to get general background information in order to best direct them to the appropriate division. 12.____
A clerk comes to your office and says that a prospective client has just called her some rather unpleasant names, accused her of being nosey and meddlesome, and has stated emphatically that she refuses to talk with an *underling,* meaning the clerk. The young woman is almost in tears. Of the following, what is the FIRST action you should take?

A. Immediately call the agency's protection officer, have him advise the client of the regulations, and tell her that she will be removed if she is not more polite.
B. Calm the clerk, introduce yourself to the client, and quietly discuss the agency's services, regulations, and informational needs, and request that she complete the interview with the clerk.

C. Calm the clerk, have her return and firmly advise the client of the agency's rules concerning the need for this first interview.
D. Introduce yourself to the client and advise her that without an apology to the clerk and completion of the interview, she will not be given any service.

13. A recent high school graduate has just been assigned to the unit which you supervise. Which of the following would be the LEAST desirable technique to use with this employee? 13.____

A. At any one time, give the new employee only as much detail about the job as the employee can absorb.
B. Always tell the new employee the correct procedure, then demonstrate how it is accomplished.
C. Assign the employee the same quantity and type of work that the other employees are doing to see if the employee can handle the job.
D. Assume the employee is tense and be prepared to repeat procedures and descriptions.

14. Assume that you supervise a work unit of several employees. Which of the following is LEAST essential in assuring that the goals which you set for the unit are achieved? 14.____

A. Establishing objectives and standards for the staff
B. Providing justification for disciplinary action
C. Measuring performance or progress of individuals against standards
D. Taking corrective action where performance is less than expected

15. One of the clerks you supervise is often reluctant to accept assignments and usually complains about the amount of work expected, although the other clerks with the same assignments and workload seem quite happy. 15.____
Of the following, the MOST accurate assumption that you can make about this clerk is that she

A. will require additional observation and help
B. will eventually have to be discharged or transferred
C. is incompetent
D. is overworked

Questions 16-21.

DIRECTIONS: Questions 16 through 21 are to be answered SOLELY on the basis of the airline timetable and the information appearing on the last page of this test.

Fact Situation:

An administrator wants you to purchase airline tickets for him so that he can attend a meeting being held in Chicago on Monday. He must leave from LaGuardia Airport in New York on Monday morning as late as possible but with arrival in Chicago no later than 9:00 A.M. He wishes to fly coach/economy class both ways. The meeting is due to end at 5:30 P.M., and he wishes to obtain the first plane after 6:45 P.M. going back to LaGuardia Airport. If all these requirements have been met, he would, if possible, also like to fly to and leave from Midway Airport in Chicago and go non-stop both ways.

16. You should obtain a ticket for the administrator from New York to Chicago on flight number 16.____

    A. 483 B. 201 C. 277 D. 539

17. You should obtain a ticket for the administrator from Chicago to New York on flight number 17.____

    A. 588 B. 692 C. 268 D. 334

18. The administrator decides to take limousines to and from both airports. 18.____
    If the limousine charge in Chicago is $52.50. and there is no reduced rate for a round-trip flight, what is the cost of the administrator's round-trip air fare PLUS limousine service?

    A. $827.50 B. $931.00 C. $963.00 D. $967.00

19. The administrator asked you whether he would be able to get breakfast on his flight to Chicago or whether he should go to the airport early and eat there before boarding the plane. He prefers to eat on the plane. 19.____
    Of the following, the BEST reply to make is:

    A. I will have to telephone the airport to find out
    B. You should eat at the airport
    C. A meal is served on the plane
    D. Only certain passengers get a meal on the plane

20. Of the following requests of the administrator concerning his travel arrangements, which one is IMPOSSIBLE to meet? 20.____

    A. Chicago arrival no later than 9 A.M.
    B. New York departure from LaGuardia Airport
    C. Non-stop flights both ways
    D. Chicago departure from Midway Airport

21. Suppose that it is necessary to take a first-class seat on the trip to Chicago although you have no problem reserving a coach/economy seat on the return trip. 21.____
    If there is no reduction in fare for round-trip flights, how much MORE will this trip cost than round-trip coach/ economy?

    A. $209 B. $236 C. $318 D. $636

22. Ms. X, a clerk under your supervision, has been working in the unit for a few weeks. Some of the other employees have complained to you that Ms. X has an annoying habit of constantly tapping her feet on the floor and it disturbs their work. 22.____
    The BEST thing for you to do is to

    A. ignore the complaints because the employees should be concerned only with their own habits
    B. speak with Ms. X privately and discuss the situation with her
    C. make a general announcement that employees should control their nervous habits
    D. observe Ms. X for a few weeks to see if the employees are correct, and then take action

23. Suppose you answer a telephone call from someone who states that he is a friend of one of your co-workers and needs the employee's new address in order to send an invitation. Your co-worker is on vacation but you know her address. Which of the following is the BEST action for you to take? 23.____

A. Give the caller the address but ask the caller not to mention that you are the one who gave it out.
B. Give the caller the address and leave a note for your co-worker stating what you did.
C. Tell the caller you do not know the address but will give the employee's phone number if that will help.
D. Offer to take his name and address and have your co-worker contact him.

24. Assume that you receive a telephone call in which the caller requests information which you know is posted in the office next to yours. You start to tell the caller you will transfer her call to the right office, but she interrupts you and says she has been transferred from office to office and is tired of getting a *run-around*. Of the following, the BEST thing for you to do is to 24.____

A. give the caller the phone number of the office next to yours and quickly end the conversation
B. give her the phone number of the office next to yours and tell her you will try to transfer her call
C. ask her if she wants to hold on while you get the information for her
D. tell the caller that she could have avoided the *run-around* by asking for the right office, and suggest that she come in person

25. Assume that your unit processes confidential forms which are submitted by persons seeking financial assistance. An individual comes to your office, gives you his name, and states that he would like to look over a form which he sent in about a week ago because he believes he omitted some important information. Of the following, the BEST thing for you to do FIRST is to 25.____

A. locate the proper form
B. call the individual's home telephone number to verify his identity
C. ask the individual if he has proof of his identity
D. call the security office

KEY (CORRECT ANSWERS)

1. A
2. C
3. D
4. B
5. B
6. A
7. B
8. B
9. C
10. C
11. C
12. B
13. C
14. B
15. A
16. A
17. D
18. B
19. C
20. D
21. C
22. B
23. D
24. C
25. C

CLERICAL ABILITIES

EXAMINATION SECTION

TEST 1

DIRECTIONS: Each question or incomplete statement is followed by several suggested answers or completions. Select the one that BEST answers the question or completes the statement. *PRINT THE LETTER OF THE CORRECT ANSWER IN THE SPACE AT THE RIGHT.*

Questions 1-4.

DIRECTIONS: Questions 1 through 4 are to be answered on the basis of the information given below.

The most commonly used filing system and the one that is easiest to learn is alphabetical filing. This involves putting records in an A to Z order, according to the letters of the alphabet. The name of a person is filed by using the following order: first, the surname or last name; second, the first name; third, the middle name or middle initial. For example, *Henry C. Young* is filed under *Y* and thereafter under *Young, Henry C.* The name of a company is filed in the same way. For example, *Long Cabinet Co.* is filed under *L* while *John T. Long Cabinet Co.* is filed under *L* and thereafter under *Long, John T. Cabinet Co.*

1. The one of the following which lists the names of persons in the CORRECT alphabetical order is: 1.____
   A. Mary Carrie, Helen Carrol, James Carson, John Carter
   B. James Carson, Mary Carrie, John Carter, Helen Carrol
   C. Helen Carrol, James Carson, John Carter, Mary Carrie
   D. John Carter, Helen Carrol, Mary Carrie, James Carson

2. The one of the following which lists the names of persons in the CORRECT alphabetical order is: 2.____
   A. Jones, John C.; Jones, John A.; Jones, John P.; Jones, John K.
   B. Jones, John P.; Jones, John K.; Jones, John C.; Jones, John A.
   C. Jones, John A.; Jones, John C.; Jones, John K.; Jones, John P.
   D. Jones, John K.; Jones, John C.; Jones, John A.; Jones, John P.

3. The one of the following which lists the names of the companies in the CORRECT alphabetical order is: 3.____
   A. Blane Co., Blake Co., Block Co., Blear Co.
   B. Blake Co., Blane Co., Blear Co., Block Co.
   C. Block Co., Blear Co., Blane Co., Blake Co.
   D. Blear Co., Blake Co., Blane Co., Block Co.

4. You are to return to the file an index card on *Barry C. Wayne Materials and Supplies Co.* 4.____
Of the following, the CORRECT alphabetical group that you should return the index card to is
A. A to G B. H to M C. N to S D. T to Z

Questions 5-10.

DIRECTIONS: In each of Questions 5 through 10, the names of four people are given. For each question, choose as your answer the one of the four names given which should be filed FIRST according to the usual system of alphabetical filing of names, as described in the following paragraph.

In filing names, you must start with the last name. Names are filed in order of the first letter of the last name, then the second letter, etc. Therefore, BAILY would be filed before BROWN, which would be filed before COLT. A name with fewer letters of the same type comes first, i.e., Smith before Smithe. If the last names are the same, the names are filed alphabetically by the first name. If the first name is an initial, a name with an initial would come before a first name that starts with the same letter as the initial. Therefore, I. BROWN would come before IRA BROWN. Finally, if both last name and first name are the same, the name would be filed alphabetically by the middle name, once again an initial coming before a middle name which starts with the same letter as the initial. If there is no middle name at all, the name would come before those with middle initials or names.

SAMPLE QUESTION: A. Lester Daniels
B. William Dancer
C. Nathan Danzig
D. Dan Lester

The last names beginning with D are filed before the last name beginning with L. Since DANIELS, DANCER, and DANZIG all begin with the same three letters, you must look at the fourth letter of the last name to determine which name should be filed first. C comes before I or Z in the alphabet, so DANCER is filed before DANIELS or DANZIG. Therefore, the answer to the above sample question is B.

5. A. Scott Biala 5.____
B. Mary Byala
C. Martin Baylor
D. Francis Bauer

6. A. Howard J. Black 6.____
B. Howard Black
C. J. Howard Black
D. John H. Black

7. A. Theodora Garth Kingston 7.____
B. Theadore Barth Kingston
C. Thomas Kingston
D. Thomas T. Kingston

8. A. Paulette Mary Huerta — 8.____
   B. Paul M. Huerta
   C. Paulette L. Huerta
   D. Peter A. Huerta

9. A. Martha Hunt Morgan — 9.____
   B. Martin Hunt Morgan
   C. Mary H. Morgan
   D. Martine H. Morgan

10. A. James T. Meerschaum — 10.____
    B. James M. Mershum
    C. James F. Mearshaum
    D. James N. Meshum

Questions 11-14.

DIRECTIONS: Questions 11 through 14 are to be answered SOLELY on the basis of the following information.

You are required to file various documents in file drawers which are labeled according to the following pattern:

DOCUMENTS

MEMOS		LETTERS	
File	Subject	File	Subject
84PM1	(A-L)	84PC1	(A-L)
84PM2	(M-Z)	84PC2	(M-Z)

REPORTS		INQUIRIES	
File	Subject	File	Subject
84PR1	(A-L)	84PQ1	(A-L)
84PR2	(M-Z)	84PQ2	(M-Z)

11. A letter dealing with a burglary should be filed in the drawer labeled — 11.____
    A. 84PM1 B. 84PC1 C. 84PR1 D. 84PQ2

12. A report on Statistics should be found in the drawer labeled — 12.____
    A. 84PM1 B. 84PC2 C. 84PR2 D. 84PQS

13. An inquiry is received about parade permit procedures. It should be filed in the drawer labeled — 13.____
    A. 84PM2 B. 84PC1 C. 84PR1 D. 84PQ2

14. A police officer has a question about a robbery report you filed. You should pull this file from the drawer labeled — 14.____
    A. 84PM1 B. 84PM2 C. 84PR1 D. 84PR2

Questions 15-22.

DIRECTIONS: Each of Questions 15 through 22 consists of four or six numbered names. For each question, choose the option (A, B, C, or D) which indicates the order in which the names should be filed in accordance with the following filing instructions:

- File alphabetically according to last name, then first name, then middle initial.
- File according to each successive letter within a name.
- When comparing two names in which the letters in the longer name are identical to the corresponding letters in the shorter name, the shorter name is filed first.
- When the last names are the same, initials are always filed before names beginning with the same letter.

15. I. Ralph Robinson
II. Alfred Ross
III. Luis Robles
IV. James Roberts

15.____

The CORRECT filing sequence for the above names should be
A. IV, II, I, III B. I, IV, III, II C. III, IV, I, II D. IV, I, III, II

16. I. Irwin Goodwin
II. Inez Gonzalez
III. Irene Goodman
IV. Ira S. Goodwin
V. Ruth I. Goldstein
VI. M.B. Goodman

16.____

The CORRECT filing sequence for the above names should be
A. V, II, I, IV, III, VI B. V, II, VI, III, IV, I
C. V, II, III, VI, IV, I D. V, II, III, VI, I, IV

17. I. George Allan
II. Gregory Allen
III. Gary Allen
IV. George Allen

17.____

The CORRECT filing sequence for the above names should be
A. IV, III, I, II B. I, IV, II, III C. III, IV, I, II D. I, III, IV, II

18. I. Simon Kauffman 18.____
II. Leo Kaufman
III. Robert Kaufmann
IV. Paul Kauffmann

The CORRECT filing sequence for the above names should be
A. I, IV, II, III B. II, IV, III, I C. III, II, IV, I D. I, II, III, IV

19. I. Roberta Williams 19.____
II. Robin Wilson
III. Roberta Wilson
IV. Robin Williams

The CORRECT filing sequence for the above names should be
A. III, II, IV, I B. I, IV, III, II C. I, II, III, IV D. III, I, II, IV

20. I. Lawrence Shultz 20.____
II. Albert Schultz
III. Theodore Schwartz
IV. Thomas Schwarz
V. Alvin Schultz
VI. Leonard Shultz

The CORRECT filing sequence for the above names should be
A. II, V, III, IV, I, VI B. IV, III, V, I, II, VI
C. II, V, I, VI, III, IV D. I, VI, II, V, III, IV

21. I. McArdle 21.____
II. Mayer
III. Maletz
IV. McNiff
V. Meyer
VI. MacMahon

The CORRECT filing sequence for the above names should be
A. I, IV, VI, III, II, V B. II, I, IV, VI, III, V
C. VI, III, II, I, IV, V D. VI, III, II, V, I, IV

22. I. Jack E. Johnson 22.____
II. R.H. Jackson
III. Bertha Jackson
IV. J.T. Johnson
V. Ann Johns
VI. John Jacobs

The CORRECT filing sequence for the above names should be
A. II, III, VI, V, IV, I B. III, II, VI, V, IV, I
C. VI, II, III, I, V, IV D. III, II, VI, IV, V, I

Questions 23-30.

DIRECTIONS: The code table below shows 10 letters with matching numbers. For each question, there are three sets of letters. Each set of letters is followed by a set of numbers which may or may not match their correct letter according to the code table. For each question, check all three sets of letters and numbers and mark your answer:

A. if no pairs are correctly matched
B. if only one pair is correctly matched
C. if only two pairs are correctly matched
D. if all three pairs are correctly matched

CODE TABLE

T	M	V	D	S	P	R	G	B	H
1	2	3	4	5	6	7	8	9	0

SAMPLE QUESTION: TMVDSP – 123456
RGBHTM – 789011
DSPRGB – 256789

In the sample question above, the first set of numbers correctly match its set of letters. But the second and third pairs contain mistakes. In the second pair, M is correctly matched with number 1. According to the code table, letter M should be correctly matched with number 2. In the third pair, the letter D is incorrectly matched with number 2. According to the code table, letter D should be correctly matched with number 4. Since only one of the pairs is correctly matched, the answer to this sample question is B.

23. RSBMRM – 759262
GDSRVH – 845730
VDBRTM - 349713
23.____

24. TGVSDR – 183247
SMHRDP – 520647
TRMHSR - 172057
24.____

25. DSPRGM – 456782
MVDBHT – 234902
HPMDBT - 062491
25.____

26. BVPTRD – 936184
GDPHMB – 807029
GMRHMV - 827032
26.____

27. MGVRSH – 283750
TRDMBS – 174295
SPRMGV - 567283
27.____

28. SGBSDM – 489542 28.____
MGHPTM – 290612
MPBMHT - 269301

29. TDPBHM – 146902 29.____
VPBMRS – 369275
GDMBHM - 842902

30. MVPTBV – 236194 30.____
PDRTMB – 47128
BGTMSM - 981232

KEY (CORRECT ANSWERS)

1.	A	11.	B	21.	C
2.	C	12.	C	22.	B
3.	B	13.	D	23.	B
4.	D	14.	D	24.	B
5.	D	15.	D	25.	C
6.	B	16.	C	26.	A
7.	B	17.	D	27.	D
8.	B	18.	A	28.	A
9.	A	19.	B	29.	D
10.	C	20.	A	30.	A

TEST 2

DIRECTIONS: Each question or incomplete statement is followed by several suggested answers or completions. Select the one that BEST answers the question or completes the statement. *PRINT THE LETTER OF THE CORRECT ANSWER IN THE SPACE AT THE RIGHT.*

Questions 1-10.

DIRECTIONS: Questions 1 through 10 each consists of two columns, each containing four lines of names, numbers and/or addresses. For each question, compare the lines in Column I with the lines in Column II to see if they match exactly, and mark your answer A, B, C, or D, according to the following instructions:

A. all four lines match exactly
B. only three lines match exactly
C. only two lines match exactly
D. only one line matches exactly

		COLUMN I	COLUMN II	
1.	I.	Earl Hodgson	Earl Hodgson	1.____
	II.	1409870	1408970	
	III.	Shore Ave.	Schore Ave.	
	IV.	Macon Rd.	Macon Rd.	
2.	I.	9671485	9671485	2.____
	II.	470 Astor Court	470 Astor Court	
	III.	Halprin, Phillip	Halperin, Phillip	
	IV.	Frank D. Poliseo	Frank D. Poliseo	
3.	I.	Tandem Associates	Tandom Associates	3.____
	II.	144-17 Northern Blvd.	144-17 Northern Blvd.	
	III.	Alberta Forchi	Albert Forchi	
	IV.	Kings Park, NY 10751	Kings Point, NY 10751	
4.	I.	Bertha C. McCormack	Bertha C. McCormack	4.____
	II.	Clayton, MO	Clayton, MO	
	III.	976-4242	976-4242	
	IV.	New City, NY 10951	New City, NY 10951	
5.	I.	George C. Morill	George C. Morrill	5.____
	II.	Columbia, SC 29201	Columbia, SD 29201	
	III.	Louis Ingham	Louis Ingham	
	IV.	3406 Forest Ave.	3406 Forest Ave.	
6.	I.	506 S. Elliott Pl.	506 S. Elliott Pl.	6.____
	II.	Herbert Hall	Hurbert Hall	
	III.	4712 Rockaway Pkway	4712 Rockaway Pkway	
	IV.	169 E. 7 St.	169 E. 7 St.	

7.	I.	345 Park Ave.	345 Park Pl.	7.____
	II.	Colman Oven Corp.	Coleman Oven Corp.	
	III.	Robert Conte	Robert Conti	
	IV.	6179846	6179846	
8.	I.	Grigori Schierber	Grigori Schierber	8.____
	II.	Des Moines, Iowa	Des Moines, Iowa	
	III.	Gouverneur Hospital	Gouverneur Hospital	
	IV.	91-35 Cresskill Pl.	91-35 Cresskill Pl.	
9.	I.	Jeffery Janssen	Jeffrey Janssen	9.____
	II.	8041071	8041071	
	III.	40 Rockefeller Plaza	40 Rockafeller Plaza	
	IV.	407 6 St.	406 7 St.	
10.	I.	5971996	5871996	10.____
	II.	3113 Knickerbocker Ave.	31123 Knickerbocker Ave.	
	III.	8434 Boston Post Rd.	8424 Boston Post Rd.	
	IV.	Penn Station	Penn Station	

Questions 11-14.

DIRECTIONS: Questions 11 through 14 are to be answered by looking at the four groups of names and addresses listed below (I, II, III, and IV), and then finding out the number of groups that have their corresponding numbered lies exactly the same.

	GROUP I	GROUP II
Line 1.	Richmond General Hospital	Richman General Hospital
Line 2.	Geriatric Clinic	Geriatric Clinic
Line 3.	3975 Paerdegat St.	3975 Peardegat St.
Line 4.	Loudonville, New York 11538	Londonville, New York 11538

	GROUP III	GROUP IV
Line 1.	Richmond General Hospital	Richmend General Hospital
Line 2.	Geriatric Clinic	Geriatric Clinic
Line 3.	3795 Paerdegat St.	3975 Paerdegat St.
Line 4.	Loudonville, New York 11358	Loudonville, New York 11538

1. In how many groups is line one exactly the same? 11.____
   A. Two B. Three C. Four D. None

12. In how many groups is line two exactly the same? 12.____
   A. Two B. Three C. Four D. None

13. In how many groups is line three exactly the same? 13.____
   A. Two B. Three C. Four D. None

14. In how many groups is line four exactly the same? 14.____
    A. Two B. Three C. Four D. None

Questions 15-18.

DIRECTIONS: Each of Questions 15 through 18 has two lists of names and addresses. Each list contains three sets of names and addresses. Check each of the three sets in the list on the right to see if they are the same as the corresponding set in the list on the left. Mark your answers:
A. if none of the sets in the right list are the same as those in the left list
B. if only one of the sets in the right list is the same as those in the left list
C. if only two of the sets in the right list are the same as those in the left list
D. if all three sets in the right list are the same as those in the left list

15.	Mary T. Berlinger 2351 Hampton St. Monsey, N.Y. 20117	Mary T. Berlinger 2351 Hampton St. Monsey, N.Y. 20117	15.____
	Eduardo Benes 483 Kingston Avenue Central Islip, N.Y. 11734	Eduardo Benes 473 Kingston Avenue Central Islip, N.Y. 11734	
	Alan Carrington Fuchs 17 Gnarled Hollow Road Los Angeles, CA 91635	Alan Carrington Fuchs 17 Gnarled Hollow Road Los Angeles, CA 91685	
16.	David John Jacobson 178 34 St. Apt. 4C New York, N.Y. 00927	David John Jacobson 178 53 St. Apt. 4C New York, N.Y. 00927	16.____
	Ann-Marie Calonella 7243 South Ridge Blvd. Bakersfield, CA 96714	Ann-Marie Calonella 7243 South Ridge Blvd. Bakersfield, CA 96714	
	Pauline M. Thompson 872 Linden Ave. Houston, Texas 70321	Pauline M. Thomson 872 Linden Ave. Houston, Texas 70321	
17.	Chester LeRoy Masterton 152 Lacy Rd. Kankakee, Ill. 54532	Chester LeRoy Masterson 152 Lacy Rd. Kankakee, Ill. 54532	17.____
	William Maloney S. LaCrosse Pla. Wausau, Wisconsin 52136	William Maloney S. LaCross Pla. Wausau, Wisconsin 52146	
	Cynthia V. Barnes 16 Pines Rd. Greenpoint, Miss. 20376	Cynthia V. Barnes 16 Pines Rd. Greenpoint,, Miss. 20376	

18.	Marcel Jean Frontenac 8 Burton On The Water Calender, Me. 01471	Marcel Jean Frontenac 6 Burton On The Water Calender, Me. 01471	18.____
	J. Scott Marsden 174 S. Tipton St. Cleveland, Ohio	J. Scott Marsden 174 Tipton St. Cleveland, Ohio	
	Lawrence T. Haney 171 McDonough St. Decatur, Ga. 31304	Lawrence T. Haney 171 McDonough St. Decatur, Ga. 31304	

Questions 19-26.

DIRECTIONS: Each of Questions 19 through 26 has two lists of numbers. Each list contains three sets of numbers. Check each of the three sets in the list on the right to see if they are the same as the corresponding set in the list on the left. Mark your answers:

A. if none of the sets in the right list are the same as those in the left list
B. if only one of the sets in the right list is the same as those in the left list
C. if only two of the sets in the right list are the same as those in the left list
D. if all three sets in the right list are the same as those in the left lists

19.	7354183476 4474747744 5791430231	7354983476 4474747774 57914302311	19.____
20.	7143592185 8344517699 9178531263	7143892185 8344518699 9178531263	20.____
21.	2572114731 8806835476 8255831246	257214731 8806835476 8255831246	21.____
22.	331476853821 6976658532996 3766042113715	331476858621 6976655832996 3766042113745	22.____
23.	8806663315 74477138449 211756663666	88066633115 74477138449 211756663666	23.____

24.	990006966996 53022219743 4171171117717	99000696996 53022219843 4171171177717	24.____
25.	24400222433004 5300030055000355 20000075532002022	24400222433004 5300030055500355 20000075532002022	25.____
26.	611166640660001116 7111300117001100733 26666446664476518	61116664066001116 7111300117001100733 26666446664476518	26.____

Questions 27-30.

DIRECTIONS: Questions 27 through 30 are to be answered by picking the answer which is in the correct numerical order, from the lowest number to the highest number, in each question.

27. A. 44533, 44518, 44516, 44547 27.____
B. 44516, 44518, 44533, 44547
C. 44547, 44533, 44518, 44516
D. 44518, 44516, 44547, 44533

28. A. 95587, 95593, 95601, 95620 28.____
B. 95601, 95620, 95587, 95593
C. 95593, 95587, 95601. 95620
D. 95620, 95601, 95593, 95587

29. A. 232212, 232208, 232232, 232223 29.____
B. 232208, 232223, 232212, 232232
C. 232208, 232212, 232223, 232232
D. 232223, 232232, 232208, 232208

30. A. 113419, 113521, 113462, 113462 30.____
B. 113588, 113462, 113521, 113419
C. 113521, 113588, 113419, 113462
D. 113419, 113462, 113521, 113588

KEY (CORRECT ANSWERS)

1.	C	11.	A	21.	C
2.	B	12.	C	22.	A
3.	D	13.	A	23.	D
4.	A	14.	A	24.	A
5.	C	15.	C	25.	C
6.	B	16.	B	26.	C
7.	D	17.	B	27.	B
8.	A	18.	B	28.	A
9.	D	19.	B	29.	C
10.	C	20.	B	30.	D

RECORD KEEPING
EXAMINATION SECTION
TEST 1

DIRECTIONS: Each question or incomplete statement is followed by several suggested answers or completions. Select the one that BEST answers the question or completes the statement. *PRINT THE LETTER OF THE CORRECT ANSWER IN THE SPACE AT THE RIGHT.*

Questions 1-7.

DIRECTIONS: In answering Questions 1 through 7, use the following master list. For each question, determine where the name would fit on the master list. Each answer choice indicates right before or after the name in the answer choice.

Aaron, Jane
Armstead, Brendan
Bailey, Charles
Dent, Ricardo
Grant, Mark
Mars, Justin
Methieu, Justine
Parker, Cathy
Sampson, Suzy
Thomas, Heather

1. Schmidt, William 1.____
   A. Right before Cathy Parker
   B. Right after Heather Thomas
   C. Right after Suzy Sampson
   D. Right before Ricardo Dent

2. Asanti, Kendall 2.____
   A. Right before Jane Aaron
   B. Right after Charles Bailey
   C. Right before Justine Methieu
   D. Right after Brendan Armstead

3. O'Brien, Daniel 3.____
   A. Right after Justine Methieu
   B. Right before Jane Aaron
   C. Right after Mark Grant
   D. Right before Suzy Sampson

4. Marrow, Alison 4.____
   A. Right before Cathy Parker
   B. Right before Justin Mars
   C. Right before Mark Grant
   D. Right after Heather Thomas

5. Grantt, Marissa 5.____
   A. Right before Mark Grant
   B. Right after Mark Grant
   C. Right after Justin Mars
   D. Right before Suzy Sampson

6. Thompson, Heath 6.____
   A. Right after Justin Mars
   B. Right before Suzy Sampson
   C. Right after Heather Thomas
   D. Right before Cathy Parker

DIRECTIONS: Before answering Question 7, add in all of the names from Questions 1 through 6. Then fit the name in alphabetical order based on the new list.

7. Francisco, Mildred 7.____
   A. Right before Mark Grant
   B. Right after Marissa Grantt
   C. Right before Alison Marrow
   D. Right after Kendall Asanti

Questions 8-10.

DIRECTIONS: In answering Questions 8 through 10, compare each pair of names and addresses. Indicate whether they are the same or different in any way.

8. William H. Pratt, J.D.
Attourney at Law — William H. Pratt, J.D.
Attorney at Law 8.____
   A. No differences
   B. 1 difference
   C. 2 differences
   D. 3 differences

9. 1303 Theater Drive,; Apt. 3-B — 1330 Theatre Drive,; Apt. 3-B 9.____
   A. No differences
   B. 1 difference
   C. 2 differences
   D. 3 differences

10. Petersdorff, Briana and Mary — Petersdorff, Briana and Mary 10.____
   A. No differences
   B. 1 difference
   C. 2 differences
   D. 3 differences

11. Which of the following words, if any, are misspelled? 11.____
   A. Affordable
   B. Circumstansial
   C. Legalese
   D. None of the above

Questions 12-13.

DIRECTIONS: Questions 12 and 13 are to be answered on the basis of the following table.

Standardized Test Results for High School Students in District #1230

	English	Math	Science	Reading
High School 1	21	22	15	18
High School 2	12	16	13	15
High School 3	16	18	21	17
High School 4	19	14	15	16

The scores for each high school in the district were averaged out and listed for each subject tested. Scores of 0-10 are significantly below College Readiness Standards. 11-15 are below College Readiness, 16-20 meet College Readiness, and 21-25 are above College Readiness.

12. If the high schools need to meet or exceed in at least half the categories in order to NOT be considered "at risk," which schools are considered "at risk"? 12.____
    A. High School 2
    B. High School 3
    C. High School 4
    D. Both A and C

13. What percentage of subjects did the district as a whole meet or exceed College Readiness standards? 13.____
    A. 25%
    B. 50%
    C. 75%
    D. 100%

Questions 14-15.

DIRECTIONS: Questions 14 and 15 are to be answered on the basis of the following information.

You have seven employees working as a part of your team: Austin, Emily, Jeremy, Christina, Martin, Harriet, and Steve. You have just sent an e-mail informing them that there will be a mandatory training session next week. To ensure that work still gets done, you are offering the training twice during the week: once on Tuesday and also on Thursday. This way half the employees will still be working while the other half attend the training. The only other issue is that Jeremy doesn't work on Tuesdays and Harriet doesn't work on Thursdays due to compressed work schedules.

14. Which of the following is a possible attendance roster for the first training session? 14.____
    A. Emily, Jeremy, Steve
    B. Steve, Christina, Harriet
    C. Harriet, Jeremy, Austin
    D. Steve, Martin, Jeremy

15. If Harriet, Christina, and Steve attend the training session on Tuesday, which of the following is a possible roster for Thursday's training session? 15.____
    A. Jeremy, Emily, and Austin
    B. Emily, Martin, and Harriet
    C. Austin, Christina, and Emily
    D. Jeremy, Emily, and Steve

Questions 16-20.

DIRECTIONS: In answering Questions 16 through 20, you will be given a word and will need to choose the answer choice that is MOST similar or different to the word.

16. Which word means the SAME as *annual*? 16.____
    A. Monthly
    B. Usually
    C. Yearly
    D. Constantly

17. Which word means the SAME as *effort*? 17.____
    A. Energy
    B. Equate
    C. Cherish
    D. Commence

18. Which word means the OPPOSITE of *forlorn*? 18.____
    A. Neglected
    B. Lethargy
    C. Optimistic
    D. Astonished

19. Which word means the SAME as *risk*? 19.____
    A. Admire
    B. Hazard
    C. Limit
    D. Hesitant

20. Which word means the OPPOSITE of *translucent*? 20.____
    A. Opaque B. Transparent C. Luminous D. Introverted

21. Last year, Jamie's annual salary was $50,000. Her boss called her today to inform her that she would receive a 20% raise for the upcoming year. How much more money will Jamie receive next year? 21.____
    A. $60,000 B. $10,000 C. $1,000 D. $51,000

22. You and a co-worker work for a temp hiring agency as part of their office staff. You both are given 6 days off per month. How many days off are you and your co-worker given in a year? 22.____
    A. 24 B. 72 C. 144 D. 48

23. If Margot makes $34,000 per year and she works 40 hours per week for all 52 weeks, what is her hourly rate? 23.____
    A. $16.34/hour B. $17.00/hour C. $15.54/hour D. $13.23/hour

24. How many dimes are there in $175.00? 24.____
    A. 175 B. 1,750 C. 3,500 D. 17,500

25. If Janey is three times as old as Emily, and Emily is 3, how old is Janey? 25.____
    A. 6 B. 9 C. 12 D. 15

KEY (CORRECT ANSWERS)

1.	C	11.	B
2.	D	12.	A
3.	A	13.	D
4.	B	14.	B
5.	B	15.	A
6.	C	16.	C
7.	A	17.	A
8.	B	18.	C
9.	C	19.	B
10.	A	20.	A

21.	B
22.	C
23.	A
24.	B
25.	B

TEST 2

DIRECTIONS: Each question or incomplete statement is followed by several suggested answers or completions. Select the one that BEST answers the question or completes the statement. *PRINT THE LETTER OF THE CORRECT ANSWER IN THE SPACE AT THE RIGHT.*

Questions 1-6.

DIRECTIONS: Questions 1 through 6 are to be answered on the basis of the following information.

item	name of item to be ordered
quantity	minimum number that can be ordered
beginning amount	amount in stock at start of month
amount received	amount receiving during month
ending amount	amount in stock at end of month
amount used	amount used during month
amount to order	will need at least as much of each item as used in the previous month
unit price	cost of each unit of an item
total price	total price for the order

Item	Quantity	Beginning	Received	Ending	Amount Used	Amount to Order	Unit Price	Total Price
Pens	10	22	10	8	24	20	$0.11	$2.20
Spiral notebooks	8	30	13	12			$0.25	
Binder clips	2 boxes	3 boxes	1 box	1 box			$1.79	
Sticky notes	3 packs	12 packs	4 packs	2 packs			$1.29	
Dry erase markers	1 pack (dozen)	34 markers	8 markers	40 markers			$16.49	
Ink cartridges (printer)	1 cartridge	3 cartridges	1 cartridge	2 cartridges			$79.99	
Folders	10 folders	25 folders	15 folders	10 folders			$1.08	

1. How many packs of sticky notes were used during the month? 1.____
   A. 16 B. 10 C. 12 D. 14

2. How many folders need to be ordered for next month? 2.____
   A. 15 B. 20 C. 30 D. 40

3. What is the total price of notebooks that you will need to order? 3.____
   A. $6.00 B. $0.25 C. $4.50 D. $2.75

4. Which of the following will you spend the second most money on? 4.____
   A. Ink cartridges
   B. Dry erase markers
   C. Sticky notes
   D. Binder clips

5. How many packs of dry erase markers should you order? 5.____
   A. 1 B. 8 C. 12 D. 0

6. What will be the total price of the file folders you order? 6.____
A. $20.16 B. $21.60 C. $10.80 D. $4.32

Questions 7-11.

DIRECTIONS: Questions 7 through 11 are to be answered on the basis of the following table.

Number of Car Accidents, By Location and Cause, for 2014						
	Location 1		Location 2		Location 3	
Cause	Number	Percent	Number	Percent	Number	Percent
Severe Weather	10		25		30	
Excessive Speeding	20	40	5		10	
Impaired Driving	15		15	25	8	
Miscellaneous	5		15		2	4
TOTALS	50	100	60	100	50	100

7. Which of the following is the third highest cause of accidents for all three locations? 7.____
A. Severe Weather
B. Impaired Driving
C. Miscellaneous
D. Excessive Speeding

8. The average number of Severe Weather accidents per week at Location 3 for the year (52 weeks) was MOST NEARLY 8.____
A. 0.57 B. 30 C. 1 D. 1.25

9. Which location had the LARGEST percentage of accidents caused by Impaired Driving? 9.____
A. 1 B. 2 C. 3 D. Both A and B

10. If one-third of the accidents at all three locations resulted in at least one fatality, what is the LEAST amount of deaths caused by accidents last year? 10.____
A. 60 B. 106 C. 66 D. 53

11. What is the percentage of accidents caused by miscellaneous means from all three locations in 2014? 11.____
A. 5% B. 10% C. 13% D. 25%

12. How many pairs of the following groups of letters are exactly alike? 12.____

ACDOBJ	ACDBOJ
HEWBWR	HEWRWB
DEERVS	DEERVS
BRFQSX	BRFQSX
WEYRVB	WEYRVB
SPQRZA	SQRPZA

A. 2 B. 3 C. 4 D. 5

Questions 13-19.

DIRECTIONS: Questions 13 through 19 are to be answered on the basis of the following information.

In 2012, the most current information on the American population was finished. The information was compiled by 200 volunteers in each of the 50 states. The territory of Puerto Rico, a sovereign of the United States, had 25 people assigned to compile data. In February of 2010, volunteers in each state and sovereign began collecting information. In Puerto Rico, data collection finished by January 31st, 2011, while work in the United States was completed on June 30, 2012. Each volunteer gathered data on the population of their state or sovereign. When the information was compiled, volunteers sent reports to the nation's capital, Washington, D.C. Each volunteer worked 20 hours per month and put together 10 reports per month. After the data was compiled in total, 50 people reviewed the data and worked from January 2012 to December 2012.

13. How many reports were generated from February 2010 to April 2010 in Illinois and Ohio? 13.____
A. 3,000 B. 6,000 C. 12,000 D. 15,000

14. How many volunteers in total collected population data in January 2012? 14.____
A. 10,000 B. 2,000 C. 225 D. 200

15. How many reports were put together in May 2012? 15.____
A. 2,000 B. 50,000 C. 100,000 D. 100,250

16. How many hours did the Puerto Rican volunteers work in the fall (September-November)? 16.____
A. 60 B. 500 C. 1,500 D. 0

17. How many workers were compiling or reviewing data in July 2012? 17.____
A. 25 B. 50 C. 200 D. 250

18. What was the total amount of hours worked by Nevada volunteers in July 2010? 18.____
A. 500 B. 4,000 C. 4,500 D. 5,000

19. How many reviewers worked in January 2013? 19.____
A. 75 B. 50 C. 0 D. 25

20. John has to file 10 documents per shelf. How many documents would it take for John to fill 40 shelves? 20.____
A. 40 B. 400 C. 4,500 D. 5,000

21. Jill wants to travel from New York City to Los Angeles by bike, which is approximately 2,772 miles. How many miles per day would Jill need to average if she wanted to complete the trip in 4 weeks? 21.____
A. 100 B. 89 C. 99 D. 94

22. If there are 24 CPU's and only 7 monitors, how many more monitors do you need to have the same amount of monitors as CPU's? 22.____
    A. Not enough information
    B. 17
    C. 31
    D. 0

23. If Gerry works 5 days a week and 8 hours each day, and John works 3 days a week and 10 hours each day, how many more hours per year will Gerry work than John? 23.____
    A. They work the same amount of hours.
    B. 450
    C. 520
    D. 832

24. Jimmy gets transferred to a new office. The new office has 25 employees, but only 16 are there due to a blizzard. How many coworkers was Jimmy able to meet on his first day? 24.____
    A. 16
    B. 25
    C. 9
    D. 7

25. If you do a fundraiser for charities in your area and raise $500 total, how much would you give to each charity if you were donating equal amounts to 3 of them? 25.____
    A. $250.00
    B. $167.77
    C. $50.00
    D. $111.11

KEY (CORRECT ANSWERS)

1.	D	11.	C
2.	B	12.	B
3.	A	13.	C
4.	C	14.	A
5.	D	15.	C
6.	B	16.	C
7.	D	17.	B
8.	A	18.	B
9.	A	19.	C
10.	D	20.	B

21.	C
22.	B
23.	C
24.	A
25.	B

TEST 3

DIRECTIONS: Each question or incomplete statement is followed by several suggested answers or completions. Select the one that BEST answers the question or completes the statement. *PRINT THE LETTER OF THE CORRECT ANSWER IN THE SPACE AT THE RIGHT.*

Questions 1-3.

DIRECTIONS: In answering Questions 1 through 3, choose the correctly spelled word.

1. A. allusion B. alusion C. allusien D. allution 1.____

2. A. altitude B. alltitude C. atlitude D. altlitude 2.____

3. A. althogh B. allthough C. althrough D. although 3.____

Questions 4-9.

DIRECTIONS: In answering Questions 4 through 9, choose the answer that BEST completes the analogy.

4. Odometer is to mileage as compass is to 4.____
   A. speed B. needle C. hiking D. direction

5. Marathon is to race as hibernation is to 5.____
   A. winter B. dream C. sleep D. bear

6. Cup is to coffee as bowl is to 6.____
   A. dish B. spoon C. food D. soup

7. Flow is to river as stagnant is to 7.____
   A. pool B. rain C. stream D. canal

8. Paw is to cat as hoof is to 8.____
   A. lamb B. horse C. lion D. elephant

9. Architect is to building as sculptor is to 9.____
   A. museum B. chisel C. stone D. statue

Questions 10-14.

DIRECTIONS: Questions 10 through 14 are to be answered on the basis of the following graph.

Population of Carroll City Broken Down by Age and Gender (in Thousands)			
Age	Female	Male	Total
Under 15	60	60	120
15-23		22	
24-33		20	44
34-43	13	18	31
44-53	20		67
64 and Over	65	65	130
TOTAL	230	232	462

10. How many people in the city are between the ages of 15-23? 10.____
    A. 70 B. 46,000 C. 70,000 D. 225,000

11. Approximately what percentage of the total population of the city was female aged 24-33? 11.____
    A. 10% B. 5% C. 15% D. 25%

12. If 33% of the males have a job and 55% of females don't have a job, which of the following statements is TRUE? 12.____
    A. Males have approximately 2,600 more jobs than females.
    B. Females have approximately 49,000 more jobs than males.
    C. Females have approximately 26,000 more jobs than males.
    D. None of the above statements are true.

13. How many females between the ages of 15-23 live in Carroll City? 13.____
    A. 67,000 B. 24,000 C. 48,000 D. 91,000

14. Assume all males 44-53 living in Carroll City are employed. If two-thirds of males age 44-53 work jobs outside of Carroll City, how many work within city limits? 14.____
    A. 31,333
    B. 15,667
    C. 47,000
    D. Cannot answer the question with the information provided

Questions 15-16.

DIRECTIONS: Questions 15 and 16 are labeled as shown. Alphabetize them for filing. Choose the answer that correctly shows the order.

15. (1) AED 15.____
(2) OOS
(3) FOA
(4) DOM
(5) COB

A. 2-5-4-3-2 B. 1-4-5-2-3 C. 1-5-4-2-3 D. 1-5-4-3-2

16. Alphabetize the names of the people. Last names are given last. 16.____
(1) Lindsey Jamestown
(2) Jane Alberta
(3) Ally Jamestown
(4) Allison Johnston
(5) Lyle Moreno

A. 2-1-3-4-5 B. 3-4-2-1-5 C. 2-3-1-4-5 D. 4-3-2-1-5

17. Which of the following words is misspelled? 17.____
A. disgust
B. whisper
C. locale
D. none of the above

Questions 18-21.

DIRECTIONS: Questions 18 through 21 are to be answered on the basis of the following list of employees.

Robertson, Aaron
Bacon, Gina
Jerimiah, Trace
Gillette, Stanley
Jacks, Sharon

18. Which employee name would come in third in alphabetized list? 18.____
A. Robertson, Aaron
B. Jerimiah, Trace
C. Gillette, Stanley
D. Jacks, Sharon

19. Which employee's first name starts with the letter in the alphabet that is five letters after the first letter of their last name? 19.____
A. Jerimiah, Trace
B. Bacon, Gina
C. Jacks, Sharon
D. Gillette, Stanley

20. How many employees have last names that are exactly five letters long? 20.____
A. 1 B. 2 C. 3 D. 4

21. How many of the employees have either a first or last name that starts with the letter "G"? 21.____
    A. 1 B. 2 C. 4 D. 5

Questions 22-25.

DIRECTIONS: Questions 22 through 25 are to be answered on the basis of the following chart.

Bicycle Sales (Model #34JA32)							
Country	May	June	July	August	September	October	Total
Germany	34	47	45	54	56	60	296
Britain	40	44	36	47	47	46	260
Ireland	37	32	32	32	34	33	200
Portugal	14	14	14	16	17	14	89
Italy	29	29	28	31	29	31	177
Belgium	22	24	24	26	25	23	144
Total	176	198	179	206	208	207	1166

22. What percentage of the overall total was sold to the German importer? 22.____
    A. 25.3% B. 22% C. 24.1% D. 23%

23. What percentage of the overall total was sold in September? 23.____
    A. 24.1% B. 25.6% C. 17.9% D. 24.6%

24. What is the average number of units per month imported into Belgium over the first four months shown? 24.____
    A. 26 B. 20 C. 24 D. 31

25. If you look at the three smallest importers, what is their total import percentage? 25.____
    A. 35.1% B. 37.1% C. 40% D. 28%

KEY (CORRECT ANSWERS)

1. A
2. A
3. D
4. D
5. C

6. D
7. A
8. B
9. D
10. C

11. B
12. C
13. C
14. B
15. D

16. C
17. D
18. D
19. B
20. B

21. B
22. A
23. C
24. C
25. A

TEST 4

DIRECTIONS: Each question or incomplete statement is followed by several suggested answers or completions. Select the one that BEST answers the question or completes the statement. *PRINT THE LETTER OF THE CORRECT ANSWER IN THE SPACE AT THE RIGHT.*

Questions 1-6.

DIRECTIONS: In answering Questions 1 through 6, choose the sentence that represents the BEST example of English grammar.

1. A. Joey and me want to go on a vacation next week. 1.____
   B. Gary told Jim he would need to take some time off.
   C. If turning six years old, Jim's uncle would teach Spanish to him.
   D. Fax a copy of your resume to Ms. Perez and me.

2. A. Jerry stood in line for almost two hours. 2.____
   B. The reaction to my engagement was less exciting than I thought it would be.
   C. Carlos and me have done great work on this project.
   D. Two parts of the speech needs to be revised before tomorrow.

3. A. Arriving home, the alarm was tripped. 3.____
   B. Jonny is regarded as a stand up guy, a responsible parent, and he doesn't give up until a task is finished.
   C. Each employee must submit a drug test each month.
   D. One of the documents was incinerated in the explosion.

4. A. As soon as my parents get home, I told them I finished all of my chores. 4.____
   B. I asked my teacher to send me my missing work, check my absences, and how did I do on my test.
   C. Matt attempted to keep it concealed from Jenny and me.
   D. If Mary or him cannot get work done on time, I will have to split them up.

5. A. Driving to work, the traffic report warned him of an accident on Highway 47. 5.____
   B. Jimmy has performed well this season.
   C. Since finishing her degree, several job offers have been given to Cam.
   D. Our boss is creating unstable conditions for we employees.

6. A. The thief was described as a tall man with a wiry mustache weighing approximately 150 pounds. 6.____
   B. She gave Patrick and I some more time to finish our work.
   C. One of the books that he ordered was damaged in shipping.
   D. While talking on the rotary phone, the car Jim was driving skidded off the road.

Questions 7-9.

DIRECTIONS: Questions 7 through 9 are to be answered on the basis of the following graph.

Ice Lake Frozen Flight (2002-2013)		
Year	Number of Participants	Temperature (Fahrenheit)
2002	22	4°
2003	50	33°
2004	69	18°
2005	104	22°
2006	108	24°
2007	288	33°
2008	173	9°
2009	598	39°
2010	698	26°
2011	696	30°
2012	777	28°
2013	578	32°

7. Which two year span had the LARGEST difference between temperatures? 7.____
   A. 2002 and 2003
   B. 2011 and 2012
   C. 2008 and 2009
   D. 2003 and 2004

8. How many total people participated in the years after the temperature reached at least 29°? 8.____
   A. 2,295
   B. 1,717
   C. 2,210
   D. 4,543

9. In 2007, the event saw 288 participants, while in 2008 that number dropped to 173. Which of the following reasons BEST explains the drop in participants? 9.____
   A. The event had not been going on that long and people didn't know about it.
   B. The lake water wasn't cold enough to have people jump in.
   C. The temperature was too cold for many people who would have normally participated.
   D. None of the above reasons explain the drop in participants.

10. In the following list of numbers, how many times does 4 come just after 2 when 2 comes just after an odd number? 10.____
    2365247653898632488572486392424
    A. 2
    B. 3
    C. 4
    D. 5

11. Which choice below lists the letter that is as far after B as S is after N in the alphabet? 11.____
    A. G
    B. H
    C. I
    D. J

Questions 12-15.

DIRECTIONS: Questions 12 through 15 are to be answered on the basis of the following directory and list of changes.

Directory		
Name	Emp. Type	Position
Julie Taylor	Warehouse	Packer
James King	Office	Administrative Assistant
John Williams	Office	Salesperson
Ray Moore	Warehouse	Maintenance
Kathleen Byrne	Warehouse	Supervisor
Amy Jones	Office	Salesperson
Paul Jonas	Office	Salesperson
Lisa Wong	Warehouse	Loader
Eugene Lee	Office	Accountant
Bruce Lavine	Office	Manager
Adam Gates	Warehouse	Packer
Will Suter	Warehouse	Packer
Gary Lorper	Office	Accountant
Jon Adams	Office	Salesperson
Susannah Harper	Office	Salesperson

Directory Updates:

- Employee e-mail addresses will adhere to the following guidelines: lastnamefirstname@apexindustries.com (ex. Susannah Harper is harpersusannah@apexindustries.com). Currently, employees in the warehouse share one e-mail, distribution@apexindustries.com.
- The "Loader" position will now be referred to as "Specialist I"
- Adam Gates has accepted a Supervisor position within the Warehouse and is no longer a Packer. All warehouse employees report to the two Supervisors and all office employees report to the Manager.

12. Amy Jones tried to send an e-mail to Adam Gates, but it wouldn't send. Which of the following offers the BEST explanation? 12.____
    A. Amy put Adam's first name first and then his last name.
    B. Adam doesn't check his e-mail, so he wouldn't know if he received the e-mail or not.
    C. Adam does not have his own e-mail.
    D. Office employees are not allowed to send e-mails to each other.

13. How many Packers currently work for Apex Industries? 13.____
    A. 2 B. 3 C. 4 D. 5

14. What position does Lisa Wong currently hold? 14.____
    A. Specialist I
    B. Secretary
    C. Administrative Assistant
    D. Loader

15. If an employee wanted to contact the office manager, which of the following e-mails should the e-mail be sent to? 15.____
    A. officemanager@apexindustries.com
    B. brucelavine@apexindustries.com
    C. lavinebruce@apexindustries.com
    D. distribution@apexindustries.com

Questions 16-19.

DIRECTIONS: In answering Questions 16 through 19, compare the three names, numbers or addresses.

16. Smiley Yarnell   Smiley Yarnel   Smily Yarnell 16.____
    A. All three are exactly alike.
    B. The first and second are exactly alike.
    C. The second and third are exactly alike.
    D. All three are different.

17. 1583 Theater Drive   1583 Theater Drive   1583 Theatre Drive 17.____
    A. All three are exactly alike.
    B. The first and second are exactly alike.
    C. The second and third are exactly alike.
    D. All three are different.

18. 3341893212   3341893212   3341893212 18.____
    A. All three are exactly alike.
    B. The first and second are exactly alike.
    C. The second and third are exactly alike.
    D. All three are different.

19. Douglass Watkins   Douglas Watkins   Douglass Watkins 19.____
    A. All three are exactly alike.
    B. The first and third are exactly alike.
    C. The second and third are exactly alike.
    D. All three are different.

Questions 20-24.

DIRECTIONS: In answering Questions 20 through 24, you will be presented with a word. Choose the synonym that BEST represents the word in question.

20. Flexible 20.____
    A. delicate   B. inflammable   C. strong   D. pliable

21. Alternative 21.____
    A. choice   B. moderate   C. lazy   D. value

22. Corroborate
    A. examine B. explain C. verify D. explain
    22.____

23. Respiration
    A. recovery B. breathing C. sweating D. selfish
    23.____

24. Negligent
    A. lazy B. moderate C. hopeless D. lax
    24.____

25. Plumber is to Wrench as Painter is to
    A. pipe B. shop C. hammer D. brush
    25.____

KEY (CORRECT ANSWERS)

1.	D	11.	A
2.	A	12.	C
3.	D	13.	A
4.	C	14.	A
5.	B	15.	C
6.	C	16.	D
7.	C	17.	B
8.	B	18.	A
9.	C	19.	B
10.	C	20.	D

21.	A
22.	C
23.	B
24.	D
25.	D

NAME AND NUMBER CHECKING

EXAMINATION SECTION

TEST 1

DIRECTIONS: This test is designed to measure your speed/and accuracy. You are urged to work both quickly and accurately and to do correctly as many lists as you can in the time allowed. The test consists of lists or pairs of names and numbers. Count the number of IDENTICAL pairs in each list. Then, select the correct number, 1, 2, 3, 4, 5, and indicate your choice in the space at the right. Two sample questions are presented for your guidance, together with the correct solutions.

SAMPLE LIST A
Adelphi College – Adelphia College
Braxton Corp – Braxeton Corp.
Wassaic State School – Wassaic State School
Central Islip State Hospital – Central Isllip State Hospital
Greenwich House – Greenwich House

NOTE: There are only two correct pairs—Wassaic State School and Greenwich House. Therefore, the CORRECT answer is 2.

SAMPLE LIST B
78453694 – 78453684
784530 – 784530
533 – 534
67845 – 67845
2368745 – 2368755

NOTE: There are only two correct pairs—784530 and 67845. Therefore, the CORRECT answer is 2.

LIST 1 1.____

Diagnostic Clinic	– Diagnostic Clinic
Yorkville Health	– Yorkville Health
Meinhard Clinic	– Meinhart Clinic
Corlears Clinic	– Carlears Clinic
Tremont Diagnostic	– Tremont Diagnostic

LIST 2 2.____

73526	– 73526
7283627198	– 7283627198
627	– 637
728352617283	– 7283526178282
6281	– 6281

LIST 3		3.____
Jefferson Clinic	– Jeffersen Clinic	
Mott Haven Center	– Mott Havan Center	
Bronx Hospital	– Bronx Hospital	
Montefiore Hospital	– Montifeore Hospital	
Beth Isreal Hospital	– Beth Israel Hospital	
LIST 4		4.____
936271826	– 936371826	
5271	– 5291	
82637192037	– 82637192037	
527182	– 5271882	
726354256	- 72635456	
LIST 5		5.____
Trinity Hospital	– Trinity Hospital	
Central Harlem	– Centrel Harlem	
St. Luke's Hospital	– St. Lukes' Hospital	
Mt. Sinai Hospital	– Mt. Sinia Hospital	
N.Y. Dispensery	– N.Y. Dispensary	
LIST 6		6.____
725361552637	– 725361555637	
7526378	– 7526377	
6975	– 6975	
82637481028	– 82637481028	
3427	– 3429	
LIST 7		7.____
Misericordia Hospital	– Miseracordia Hospital	
Lebonan Hospital	– Lebanon Hospital	
Gouverneur Hospital	– Gouverner Hospital	
German Polyclinic	– German Policlinic	
French Hospital	– French Hospital	
LIST 8		8.____
8277364933251	– 827364933351	
63728	– 63728	
367281	– 367281	
62733846273	– 6273846293	
62836	- 6283	
LIST 9		9.____
King's County Hospital	– Kings County Hospital	
St. Johns Long Island	– St. John's Long Island	
Bellevue Hospital	– Bellvue Hospital	
Beth David Hospital	– Beth David Hospital	
Samaritan Hospital	– Samariton Hospital	

LIST 10		10.____
62836454	– 62836455	
42738267	– 42738369	
573829	– 573829	
738291627874	– 738291627874	
725	- 735	
LIST 11		11.____
Bloomingdal Clinic	– Bloomingdale Clinic	
Communitty Hospital	– Community Hospital	
Metroplitan Hospital	– Metropoliton Hospital	
Lenox Hill Hospital	– Lonex Hill Hospital	
Lincoln Hospital	– Lincoln Hospital	
LIST 12		12.____
6283364728	– 6283648	
627385	– 627383	
54283902	– 54283602	
63354	– 63354	
7283562781	- 7283562781	
LIST 13		13.____
Sydenham Hospital	– Sydanham Hospital	
Roosevalt Hospital	– Roosevelt Hospital	
Vanderbilt Clinic	– Vanderbild Clinic	
Women's Hospital	– Woman's Hospital	
Flushing Hospital	– Flushing Hospital	
LIST 14		14.____
62738	– 62738	
727355542321	– 72735542321	
263849332	– 263849332	
262837	– 263837	
47382912	- 47382922	
LIST 15		15.____
Episcopal Hospital	– Episcapal Hospital	
Flower Hospital	– Flouer Hospital	
Stuyvesent Clinic	– Stuyvesant Clinic	
Jamaica Clinic	– Jamaica Clinic	
Ridgwood Clinic	– Ridgewood Clinic	
LIST 16		16.____
628367299	– 628367399	
111	– 111	
118293304829	– 1182839489	
4448	– 4448	
333693678	- 333693678	

LIST 17		17.____
Arietta Crane Farm	– Areitta Crane Farm	
Bikur Chilim Home	– Bikur Chilom Home	
Burke Foundation	– Burke Foundation	
Blythedale Home	– Blythdale Home	
Campbell Cottages	– Cambell Cottages	
LIST 18		18.____
32123	– 32132	
273893326783	– 27389326783	
473829	– 473829	
7382937	– 7383937	
3628890122332	- 36289012332	
LIST 19		19.____
Caraline Rest	– Caroline Rest	
Loreto Rest	– Loretto Rest	
Edgewater Creche	– Edgwater Creche	
Holiday Farm	– Holiday Farm	
House of St. Giles	– House of st. Giles	
LIST 20		20.____
557286777	– 55728677	
3678902	– 3678892	
1567839	– 1567839	
7865434712	– 7865344712	
9927382	- 9927382	
LIST 21		21.____
Isabella Home	– Isabela Home	
James A. Moore Home	– James A. More Home	
The Robin's Nest	– The Roben's Nest	
Pelham Home	– Pelam Home	
St. Eleanora's Home	– St. Eleanora's Home	
LIST 22		22.____
273648293048	– 273648293048	
334	– 334	
7362536478	– 7362536478	
7362819273	– 7362819273	
7362	- 7363	
LIST 23		23.____
St. Pheobe's Mission	– St. Phebe's Mission	
Seaside Home	– Seaside Home	
Speedwell Society	– Speedwell Society	
Valeria Home	– Valera Home	
Wiltwyck	- Wildwyck	

LIST 24 24.____

63728	– 63738
63728192736	– 63728192738
428	– 458
62738291527	– 62738291529
63728192	- 63728192

LIST 25 25.____

McGaffin	– McGafin
David Ardslee	– David Ardslee
Axton Supply	– Axeton Supply Co
Alice Russell	– Alice Russell
Dobson Mfg. Co.	– Dobsen Mfg. Co.

KEY (CORRECT ANSWERS)

1.	3	11.	1
2.	3	12.	2
3.	1	13.	1
4.	1	14.	2
5.	1	15.	1
6.	2	16.	3
7.	1	17.	1
8.	2	18.	1
9.	1	19.	1
10.	2	20.	2

21.	1
22.	4
23.	2
24.	1
25.	2

TEST 2

DIRECTIONS: This test is designed to measure your speed/and accuracy. You are urged to work both quickly and accurately and to do correctly as many lists as you can in the time allowed. The test consists of lists or pairs of names and numbers. Count the number of IDENTICAL pairs in each list. Then, select the correct number, 1, 2, 3, 4, 5, and indicate your choice in the space at the right.

LIST 1 1.____

82637381028 – 82637281028
928 – 928
72937281028 – 72937281028
7362 – 7362
927382615 – 927382615

LIST 2 2.____

Albee Theatre – Albee Theatre
Lapland Lumber Co. – Laplund Lumber Co.
Adelphi College – Adelphi College
Jones & Son Inc. – Jones & Sons Inc.
S.W. Ponds Co. – S.W. Ponds Co.

LIST 3 3.____

85345 – 85345
895643278 – 895643277
726352 – 726353
632685 – 632685
7263524 – 7236524

LIST 4 4.____

Eagle Library – Eagle Library
Dodge Ltd. – Dodge Co.
Stromberg Carlson – Stromberg Carlsen
Clairice Ling – Clairice Linng
Mason Book Co. – Matson Book Co.

LIST 5 5.____

66273 – 66273
629 – 629
7382517283 – 7382517283
637281 – 639281
2738261 – 2788261

LIST 6 6.____

Robert MacColl – Robert McColl
Buick Motor – Buck Motors
Murray Bay & Co. Ltd. – Murray Bay Co. Ltd.
L.T. Ltyle – L.T. Lyttle
A.S. Landas – A.S. Landas

LIST 7		7.____
6271526374890	– 627152637490	
73526189	– 73526189	
5372	– 5392	
637281142	– 63728124	
4783946	– 4783046	
LIST 8		8.____
Tyndall Burke	– Tyndell Burke	
W. Briehl	– W. Briehl	
Burritt Publishing Co.	– Buritt Publishing Co.	
Frederick Breyer & Co.	– Frederick Breyer Co.	
Bailey Buulard	– Bailey Bullard	
LIST 9		9.____
634	– 634	
16837	– 163837	
273892223678	– 27389223678	
527182	– 527782	
3628901223	– 3629002223	
LIST 10		10.____
Ernest Boas	– Ernest Boas	
Rankin Barne	– Rankin Barnes	
Edward Appley	– Edward Appely	
Camel	– Camel	
Caiger Food Co.	– Caiger Food Co.	
LIST 11		11.____
6273	– 6273	
322	– 332	
15672839	– 15672839	
63728192637	– 63728192639	
738	– 738	
LIST 12		12.____
Wells Fargo Co.	– Wells Fargo Co.	
W.D. Brett	– W.D. Britt	
Tassco Co.	– Tassko Co.	
Republic Mills	– Republic Mill	
R.W. Burnham	– R.W. Burhnam	
LIST 13		13.____
7253529152	– 7283529152	
6283	– 6383	
52839102738	– 5283910238	
308	– 398	
82637201927	– 8263720127	

LIST 14		14.____
Schumacker Co.	– Shumacker Co.	
C.H. Caiger	– C.H. Caiger	
Abraham Strauss	– Abram Straus	
B.F. Boettjer	– B.F. Boettijer	
Cut-Rate Store	– Cut-Rate Stores	
LIST 15		15.____
15273826	– 15273826	
72537	– 73537	
726391027384	– 62639107384	
637389	– 627399	
725382910	– 725382910	
LIST 16		16.____
Hixby Ltd.	– Hixby Lt'd.	
S. Reiner	– S. Riener	
Reynard Co.	– Reynord Co.	
Esso Gassoline Co.	– Esso Gasolene Co.	
Belle Brock	– Belle Brock	
LIST 17		17.____
7245	– 7245	
819263728192	– 819263728172	
682537289	– 682537298	
789	– 789	
82936542891	– 82936542891	
LIST 18		18.____
Joseph Cartwright	– Joseph Cartwrite	
Foote Food Co.	– Foot Food Co.	
Weiman & Held	– Weiman & Held	
Sanderson Shoe Co.	– Sandersen Shoe Co.	
A.M. Byrne	– A.N. Byrne	
LIST 19		19.____
4738267	– 4738277	
63728	– 63729	
6283628901	– 6283628991	
918264	– 918264	
263728192037	– 2637728192073	
LIST 20		20.____
Exray Laboratories	– Exray Labratories	
Curley Toy Co.	– Curly Toy Co.	
J. Lauer & Cross	– J. Laeur & Cross	
Mireco Brands	– Mireco Brands	
Sandor Lorand	– Sandor Larand	

LIST 21		21.____
607	– 609	
6405	– 6403	
976	– 996	
101267	– 101267	
2065432	– 20965432	

LIST 22		22.____
John Macy & Sons	– John Macy & Son	
Venus Pencil Co.	– Venus Pencil Co.	
Nell McGinnis	– Nell McGinnis	
McCutcheon & Co.	– McCutcheon & Co.	
Sun-Tan Oil	– Sun-Tan Oil	

LIST 23		23.____
703345700	– 703345700	
46754	– 466754	
3367490	– 3367490	
3379	– 3778	
47384	– 47394	

LIST 24		24.____
arthritis	– arthritis	
asthma	– asthma	
endocrine	– endocrene	
gastro-enterological	– gastrol-enteralogical	
orthopedic	– orthopedic	

LIST 25		25.____
743829432	– 743828432	
998	– 998	
732816253902	– 732816252902	
46829	– 46830	
7439120249	– 7439210249	

KEY (CORRECT ANSWERS)

1.	4	11.	3
2.	3	12.	1
3.	2	13.	1
4.	1	14.	1
5.	2	15.	2
6.	1	16.	1
7.	2	17.	3
8.	1	18.	1
9.	1	19.	1
10.	3	20.	1

21.	1
22.	4
23.	2
24.	3
25.	1

ARITHMETICAL REASONING

EXAMINATION SECTION

TEST 1

DIRECTIONS: Each question or incomplete statement is followed by several suggested answers or completions. Select the one that BEST answers the question or completes the statement. *PRINT THE LETTER OF THE CORRECT ANSWER IN THE SPACE AT THE RIGHT.*

1. The initial mark-up in a store is 40%; mark-downs are 5%; shortages 1%; cash discounts 5%; alteration costs 5%; expenses 25%. The maintained mark-up is 1.____
   A. 34% B. 39% C. 36.4% D. 30%

2. A buyer of TV sets wishes to maintain a mark-up of 37½% after all mark-downs are taken. Of 25 sets costing $150 each, he sells 20 at $265. How much can he mark-down the remaining 5 sets and still realize his mark-up objective? 2.____
   A. $166 B. $150 C. $140 D. $125

3. An article originally selling for $12 and costing $8 was marked down to $10. Assuming the same mark-up, what is the present market value of its cost? 3.____
   A. $6.68 B. $8.00 C. $5.67 D. $6.86

4. What is the *on* percentage of trade discounts of 20% and 10%? 4.____
   A. 70 B. 85 C. 72 D. 80

5. Canadian cost of a sweater is $40. Packing and labor cost $5.00; ad valorem duty, 40%; specific duty, 65¢; rate of exchange, .9091. What is the duty in American currency? 5.____
   A. $16.96 B. $16.36 C. $18.00 D. $18.60

6. A bolt of cloth measures 40 yards. The following yardages are sold: 4½, 5¾, $6\frac{7}{8}$. How many yards are left? 6.____
   A. $23\frac{7}{8}$ B. 22½ C. $22\frac{7}{8}$ D. $24\frac{3}{8}$

7. A shirt manufacturer has 76½ yards of broadcloth to be used for shirts. If each shirt takes 2½ yards, how many shirts can he make? 7.____
   A. 38 B. 30 C. 19 D. 31

8. Subtract 1.003 from 24.5. 8.____
   A. 24.003 B. 12.42 C. 23.2 D. 23.497

9. A store carries a stock amounting to $265,830.25. Cash discounts, on the average, amount to 5¼%. 9.____
How much are the cash discounts?
A. $13,956.09 B. $1,395.61 C. $139.56 D. $1.39

10. If the sales in a department totaled $67,507.50 and the average sale was $22.50, how many transactions were there? 10.____
A. 3,000 B. 300 C. 30,000 D. 0

11. A department store reports a decrease in sales of 5.5% for this year. 11.____
If this year's sales are $275,825,000, last year's sales were
A. $291,878,000 B. $290,995,000
C. $260,655,000 D. $290,788,000

12. For the current year, the sales volume in a store was $50,000,000. Other income amounted to $1,500,000, operating expenses were $10,000,000; cost of goods sold, $37,500,000. 12.____
What is the percent of net profit based on retail?
A. 10 B. 8 C. 50 D. 13

13. If this year's sales shown an increase of 300% over last year, this year's sales are how many times last year's sales? 13.____
A. 3 B. $1\frac{1}{3}$ C. 4 D. ¼

14. Net sales in a shop amounted to $374,000; returns were 10%; allowances 5%. 14.____
What were the gross sales?
A. $430,100 B. $415,000 C. $411,400 D. $440,000

15. If the average sale in a store is expected to rise 5% over last year, and the number of transactions increases 3%, what percentage of increase in dollar sales volume should be planned? 15.____
A. 8 B. 4 C. 8.15 D. 8.51

16. The billed cost on an invoice is $300; freight charges, $10; cash discount, 2%; the retail value of the merchandise is $525. 16.____
The mark-up percent on retail is
A. 40.9 B. 42 C. 69 D. 69.5

17. A hat costing $30.00 is to be given a mark-up of 45% on retail. 17.____
The retail should be
A. $43.50 B. $46.40 C. $55.40 D. $54.50

18. Retail price $40 per unit; mark-up 40% of retail; transportation charge, $1 per unit. 18.____
Find billed cost that store can pay.
A. 23 B. $24 C. $23.75 D. $24.75

19. A buyer plans to spend $17,000 at retail for merchandise at a mark-up of 34%. He finds a special value at $3,000 that he can sell for $6,000. What mark-up percentage does he need on the balance of his purchases in order to achieve his planned 34%? 19.____
    A. 35 B. 19.9 C. 15 D. 22.5

20. A store has a gross margin of 40% and reductions of 13%. Cash discount on purchases are not credited to the department. There are no alteration costs. What is the initial mark-up? 20.____
    A. 46% B. 53% C. 27% D. 26%

21. A dress is to retail for $35 with a mark-up of 40% of retail. The cost of the dress to the retailer was 21.____
    A. $25 B. $21 C. $14 D. $20

22. The cost is $1.20 and the desired gross profit is 40% of retail. The retail price should be 22.____
    A. $1.60 B. $1.68 C. $2.00 D. $2.40

23. The realized mark-up on a TV set is $50. The mark-up is 25% of retail. The cost of the TV set to the retailer was 23.____
    A. $200 B. $125 C. $100 D. $150

24. Farnum, a salesman, earns $19.20 per hour for 40 hours a week, with time and a half for all hours over 40 per week. Last week, his total earnings were $940.80. How many hours did he work last week? 24.____
    A. 46 B. 49 C. 47 D. 48

25. Dane & Clarke, partners, share profits in a 5:3 ratio. Dane's share of the profit for this year was $12,000 more than Clarke's share. Clarke's share of the net profit was 25.____
    A. $30,000 B. $48,000 C. $36,000 D. $18,000

KEY (CORRECT ANSWERS)

1. C
2. D
3. A
4. C
5. A

6. C
7. B
8. D
9. A
10. A

11. A
12. B
13. C
14. D
15. C

16. A
17. D
18. A
19. B
20. A

21. B
22. C
23. D
24. A
25. D

SOLUTIONS TO PROBLEMS

1. 5 + 5 – 1 = 9%. Then, (40%)(91) = 36.4%.

2. (25)($150) = $3,750, and $3,750 ÷ .625 = $6000 total selling price of all sets. $6,000 – (20)($265) = $700; 700 ÷ 5 = $140 selling price for each of the last 5 sets. Markdown amount = $265 - $140 = $125.

3. When the article's original selling price was $12, its cost was $8.00. If the article's original selling price were to be $10, it would cost $(8.00)/12.00×10.00) = $6.67.

4. Resulting percentage = (1.20)(1-.10) = .72 = 72%.

5. ($45)(.40) = $18 + .65 = $18.65. Then, ($18.65)(.9091) = $16.95, closest to $16.96 in American currency.

6. 40 – 4½ - 5¾ - $6^7/_8$ = $22^7/_8$ yds.

7. 76½ ÷ 2½ = 30.6, rounded down to 30 shirts.

8. 24.5 – 1.003 = 23.497.

9. ($265,830)(.0525) = $13,956.09.

10. $67,507.50 ÷ $22.50 = 3,000 transactions.

11. $275,825,000 ÷ .945 = $291,878,000.

12. $50,000,000 + $1,500,000 - $10,000,000 = $37,500,000 = $4,000,000.
Then, $4,000,000 ÷ $50,000,000 = .08 = 8%.

13. An increase of 300% over x = 4x, so sales are 4 times as large.

14. Gross sales = $374,000 ÷ .85 = $440,000.

15. (1.05)(1.03) = 1.0815, which represents an 8.15% increase in dollar sales volume.

16. $525 - $310 = $215; then, $215/$525 = 40.9%.

17. $30 will represent 55% of retail amount. Thus, retail will be $30 ÷ .55 = $54.50.

18. ($40)(.60) - $1 = $23.

19. ($17,000)(1.34) = $22,780. Then, $22,780 - $6000 = $16,780. Also, $17,000 - $3,000 = $14,000. Finally, ($16,780 - $14,000) ÷ $14,000 ≈ 19.9%.

20. Let x = markup percent. Then, x – 40/x = .13. Solving, x = 46.

21. Cost = ($35)(.60) = $21.

22. Let x = retail price. Then, $1.20 = .60x. Solving, x = $2.00.

23. $50 = 25% of retail, so retail = $200. Thus, cost = $200 - $50 = $150.

24. Let x = overtime hours. Then, ($19.20)(40) + $28.80x = $940.80. Solving, x = 6 total.

25. 5x = 3x - $12,000. So, x = $6,000. Clarke's share = (3)($6,000) = $18,000.

TEST 2

DIRECTIONS: Each question or incomplete statement is followed by several suggested answers or completions. Select the one that BEST answers the question or completes the statement. *PRINT THE LETTER OF THE CORRECT ANSWER IN THE SPACE AT THE RIGHT.*

1. Assume that you require 77 dozen felt practice golf balls. 1.____
   Which of the following represents the LOWEST bid for these balls?
   A. 41¢ per half-dozen less a 3% discount
   B. 83¢ per dozen less a 7½% discount
   C. 85¢ per dozen less a 10% discount
   D. $65.00 less a series discount of 3%, 2%

2. Assume that you require 1,944 rulers, packed 12 to the box, 18 boxes to the carton. 2.____
   Which of the following represents the LOWEST bid for these rulers?
   A. 5½ ¢ per ruler
   B. 6¢ for the first 750 rulers; 5½¢ for the next 750 rulers; 4½¢ for every ruler thereafter
   C. $11.85 per carton
   D. $110 less series discounts of 2%, 1%.

3. Assume that you require 20 cartons of colored raffia, cellophane wrapped in one lb. packages, 50 packages to the carton. 3.____
   Which of the following represents the LOWEST bid for the raffia?
   A. 8¢ per lb.; 15¢ per carton packaging charge; 20¢ per carton delivery charge
   B. 9¢ per lb. less a 3% discount
   C. 10¢ per lb. for the first 150 lbs.; 9¢ per lb. for the next 200 lbs.; 80 for each lb. thereafter
   D. $83.50 less a 4½% discount

4. Assume that you require 50 yards of table felt, 48" wide, and 12 yards of table felt, 72" wide. 4.____
   Which of the following represents the LOWEST bid for this felt?
   A. 32¢ per yard (48" wide), 40¢ per yard (72" wide)
   B. 34¢ per yard (48" wide), 43¢ per yard (72" wide); series discounts of 5%, 3%
   C. 360 per yard (48" wide), 41¢ per yard (72" wide); 8% discount, packing charge 75¢
   D. $23.00 for the order, 9% discount, packing charge 50¢

5. If the cost of 3 erasers is 5¢, the cost of 2½ dozen erasers is 5.____
   A. 18¢ B. 37½¢ C. 50¢ D. 31½¢

6. A circle graph of a budget shows the expenditure of 26.2% for housing, 28.4% for food, 12% for clothing, 12.7% for taxes, and the balance for miscellaneous items.
The percent for miscellaneous items is
A. 31.5 B. 79.3 C. 20.7 D. 68.5 6.____

7. The cost of a broadloom rug measuring 4 feet by 6 feet, at $6.30 per square yard, is
A. $16.80 B. $50.40 C. $37.60 D. $21.00 7.____

8. The number of tiles each measuring 2 inches by 3 inches needed for a wall 3 feet high and 5 feet long is
A. 180 B. 30 C. 360 D 60 8.____

9. Assume that you require 4 tons of fertilizer. The fertilizer is packed in 100 pound bags.
Which of the following represents the LOWEST bid for the fertilizer? 9.____
A. 6¢ per pound
B. $5.50 per bag
C. $7.00 for each of the first 30 bags; $5.00 for each bag thereafter
D. $500.00 less 3½% discount

10. Assume pencils are packed 5 gross to the case. A buyer requires 3,800 pencils each for three departments and 2,700 pencils for another department. Assume that the vendor will ship unbroken cases only directly to each department.
How many cases should he buy? 10.____
A. 21 B. 22 C. 48 D. 49

11. Assume that a buyer had to purchase 40,000 lbs. of salt.
Which one of the following bids should he accept, assuming quality, service, and delivery terms are all the same? 11.____
A. 1¢ per pound, 2%-30 days
B. 99¢ per 100 lbs., 1%-30 days
C. $19 per ton, 1%-30 days
D. $18 per ton, net-30 days

12. Which one of the following four bids represent the BEST value, assuming delivery costs amount to $100? 12.____
A. $1,000 f.o.b. buyer, less 2%-10 days
B. $900 f.o.b. seller, less 2%-10 days
C. $975 delivered, net cash 30 days
D. $990 f.o.b. buyer, less 1%-10 days

13. Suppose that four suppliers make the following offers to sell 2,000 units of a particular commodity.
Which one is the MOST advantageous proposal? 13.____
A. $10 list, less 40% and 5%
B. $5 cost, plus 20% to cover overhead and profit
C. $10 list, less 20% and 20%
D. $5 cost, plus 10% overhead and 10% for profit

14. Suppose that you purchase 100 units of an item at a list of $1 per unit less 40% and 10%, and less 2% if paid within 10 days. 14.____
If payment is made within the 10-day limit, the amount of the payment should be
A. $52.92 B. $54.00 C. $58.80 D. $60.00

15. Assume that the 2018 cost of living factor was 100 and that a certain product was selling that year for $5 per unit. Assume further that at the present time the cost of living factor is 150. 15.____
If the selling price of the product increased 10% more than the cost of living during this period, at the present time the product would be selling for _____ per unit.
A. $8.25 B. $10.50 C. $16.50 D. $7.75

16. A certain food is sold in 4 ounce cans at 10 for $1.00 and in 1 pound cans at 3 for $1.00. 16.____
The savings in price per ounce by purchasing the food in the larger can is _____ cents/ounce.
A. .53 B. .35 C. .42 D. .68

17. After an article is discounted at 25%, it sells for $375. 17.____
The ORIGINAL price of the article was
A. $93.75 B. $350 C. $35 D $500

18. Assume that you require 1,440 pencils, packed 12 to the box, 24 boxes to the carton. 18.____
Which of the following represents the LOWEST bid for these pencils?
A. 2¢ per pencil
B. $6.50 per carton
C. 27¢ per box less a 4% discount
D. $40 less a 3% discount

19. If erasers cost 8¢ each for the first 250, 70 each for the next 250, and 5¢ for every eraser thereafter, how many erasers may be purchased for $50? 19.____
A. 600 B. 750 C. 850 D. 1,000

20. Assume that a buyer saves $14 on the purchase of an item that is discounted at 25% 20.____
The amount of money that the buyer must pay for the item is
A. $42 B. $52 C. $54 D. $56

Questions 21-24.

DIRECTIONS: Questions 21 through 24 are to be answered on the basis of the following method of obtaining a reorder point: multiply the monthly rate of consumption by the lead time (in months) and add the minimum balance.

21. If the lead time is one-half month, the minimum balance is 6 units, and the monthly rate of consumption is 4 units, then the reorder point is _____ units. 21.____
A. 4 B. 6 C. 8 D. 12

22. If the reorder point is 25 units, the lead time is 3 months, and the minimum balance is 10 units, then the average monthly rate of consumption is _____ units. 22.____
A. 3 B. 5 C. 6 D. 10

23. If the reorder point is 400 units, the lead time is 2 months, and the monthly rate of consumption is 150 units, then the minimum balance is _____ units. 23.____
A. 50 B. 100 C. 150 D. 200

24. If the reorder point is 75 units, the monthly rate of consumption is 60 units, and the minimum balance is 45 units, then the lead time is ______ month(s). 24.____
A. ½ B. 1 C. 2 D. 4

25. A purchasing office has 4,992 special requisitions to be processed. Working alone, Buyer A could process these in 30 days; working alone, Buyer B could process these in 40 days; working alone, Buyer C could process these in 60 days. 25.____
The LEAST number of days in which Buyers A, B, and C working together can process these 4,992 special requisitions is APPROXIMATELY _____ days.
A. 14 B. 20 C. 34 D. 45

KEY (CORRECT ANSWERS)

1. C
2. B
3. D
4. B
5. C

6. C
7. A
8. C
9. B
10. B

11. D
12. C
13. A
14. A
15. A

16. C
17. D
18. A
19. B
20. A

21. C
22. B
23. B
24. A
25. A

SOLUTIONS TO PROBLEMS

1. Bid A = (.82)(77)(.97) ≈ $61.25
   Bid B = (.83)(77)(.925) ≈ $59.12
   Bid C = (.85)(77)(.90) ≈ $58.91
   Bid D = ($65.00)(.97)(.98) ≈ $61.79.
   Thus, Bid C is lowest.

2. Bid A = (.055)(1944) = $106.92
   Bid B = (.06)(750) + (.055)(750) + (.045)(444) = $106.23
   Bid C = ($11.85)(9) = $106.65
   Bid D = ($110)(.98)(.99) ≈ $106.72.
   Thus, Bid B is lowest.

3. Bid A = (.08)(1000) + (.15)(20) + (.20)(20) = $87.00
   Bid B = (.09)(1000) = $87.30
   Bid C = (.10)(150) + (.09)(200) + (.08)(650) = $85.00
   Bid D = ($83.50)(.955) ≈ $79.74
   Thus, Bid D is lowest.

4. Bid A = (.32)(50) + (.40)(12) = $20.80
   Bid B = (.34)(50) + (.43)(12) = $22.16; so ($22.16)(.95)(.97) ≈ $20.42
   Bid C = (.36)(50) + (.41)(12) = $22.92; so ($22.92)(.92) + .75 ≈ $21.84
   Bid D = ($23.00)(.91) + .50 = $21.43
   Bid B is lowest.

5. (2½)(12) = 30 erasers, which will cost (.05)(10) = 50¢

6. 100 – 26.2 – 28.4 – 12 – 12.7 = 20.7% for miscellaneous items.

7. 24 ÷ 9 = $2^2/_3$ sq. yds. Then, ($6.30)($2^2/_3$) = $16.80

8. 3'2" = 18; 5'3" = 20. Thus, (18)(20) = 360 tiles.

9. Bid A = (.06)(8000) = $480
   Bid B = ($5.50)(80) = $440
   Bid C = ($7.00)(30) + ($5.00)(50) = $460
   Bid D = ($500)(.965) = $482.59
   Thus, Bid B is lowest.

10. 5 gross = 5(144); 3800 will be 6 unbroken cases × 3 = 18.
    2700 will be 4 unbroken cases = 4
    22

11. Bid A = (.01)(40,000)(.98) = $392.00
Bid B = (.99)(400)(.99) = $392.04
Bid C = ($19)(20)(.99) = $376.20
Bid D = ($18)(20) = $360.00
Bid D is lowest.

12. A. 1,000 – 2% = 980
B. 900 + 100 – 2% = 980
C. 975
D. 990 – 9.90 = 980.10
C is best value.

13. Proposal A: ($10)(.60)(.95) = $5.70
Proposal B: $5 + ($5)(.20) = $6.00
Proposal C: ($10)(.80)(.80) = $6.40
Proposal D: $5 + (.20)($5) = $6.00
Proposal A is lowest.

14. Payment = ($100)(.60)(.90)(.98) = $52.92

15. Present cost = ($5)(1.50)(1.10) = $8.25

16. 40 ounces for $1.00 in smaller cans means 2.5 cents per ounce. For the larger cans, (3)(16) = 48 ounces for $1.00, which means 2.083 cents per ounce. The savings is approximately .42 cents per ounce.

17. Original price = $375 ÷ 75 = $500

18. Bid A = (1440)(.02) = $28.80
Bid B = (1440 ÷ 288)($6.50) = $32.50
Bid C = [(144 ÷ 12)(.27)][.96] = $31.10
Bid D = ($40)(.97) = $38.80
Bid A is lowest.

19. 250 erasers cost (250)(.08) = $20
500 erasers cost $20 + (250)(.07) = $37.50
The number of additional erasers = ($50 - $37.50) ÷ .05 = 250
Total number of erasers = 750

20. $14 ÷ .25 = $56. Then, $56 - $14 = $42

21. (4)(.5) + 6 = 8 units

22. Let x = monthly rate. Then, (x)(3) + 10 = 25. Solving, x = 5 units.

23. Let x = minimum balance. (150)(2) + x = 400. Solving, x = 100 units.

24. Let x = lead time. (60)(x) + 45 =75. Solving, x = ½ month.

25. Buyer A does $4992 \div 30 \approx 166$ per day.
Buyer B does $4992 \div 40 \approx 125$ per day.
Buyer C does $4992 \div 60 \approx 83$ per day.
Working together, approximately 374 requisitions are done per day.
Finally, $4992 \div 374 \approx 13$, closest to 14 in selections.

www.ingramcontent.com/pod-product-compliance
Lightning Source LLC
Chambersburg PA
CBHW082047300426
44117CB00015B/2634
* 9 7 8 1 7 9 9 3 1 8 7 4 3 *